W9-CYA-890

The Manager's Guide to

ORGANIZATIONAL
ENGINEERING™

Gary J. Salton, Ph.D.
Ann Arbor, MI

HRD PRESS
Amherst, Massachusetts

Copyright© 2000, Professional Communications

Published by:
HRD Press, Inc.
22 Amherst Road
Amherst, MA 01002
800-822-2801 (U.S. and Canada)
413-253-3488
413-253-3490 (FAX)
www.hrdpress.com

All rights reserved. Any reproduction of these materials in any
media without written consent of the publisher is a violation of
international copyright law.

Editorial and production services by Mary George
Cover design by Donna Thibault-Wong

PRINTED IN CANADA

TABLE OF CONTENTS

Introduction v

1. Understanding: The Basics of
Information Processing 1

2. Measurement: Creating the Standard
OE Tool 19

3. Predicting Individual Behavior 37

4. Predicting Group Behavior 63

5. Guidance: Providing Semi-Fixed
Initiatives 87

6. Guidance: Providing Flexible
Initiatives 101

7. Materiality: Results That Make
a Difference 137

INTRODUCTION

HAVE YOU EVER WONDERED why the performance of some groups sparkles while that of other groups is barely mediocre? Have you seen teams start out spectacularly then fizzle, while others that barely got off the ground suddenly blossom? Have you ever worked with someone whom you just could not get through to? Have you witnessed situations where well thought out plans were never realized? Have you ever tried to introduce a culture change in an organizational unit only to find that your best efforts had no effect?

These and many similar questions are the subject of the new discipline of *organizational engineering,* defined below. The discipline offers a new way of looking at how people behave in groups from the dual perspectives of information-processing theory and sociological concepts.

➡ ORGANIZATIONAL ENGINEERING IS . . .

a branch of knowledge that seeks to *understand, measure, predict, and guide* the behavior of groups in a way that produces *positive results* of significant consequence and magnitude for all involved.

Organizational engineering (OE) is so named because it adopts an engineering philosophy rather than a scientific one. Engineering is a field that seeks the solution of practical issues. In addressing its objectives, engineering uses science, logic, mathematics, aesthetics, and any other branch of knowledge that allows it to better accomplish its ends. The results it produces are repeatable and usually of significant consequence to the issue being addressed.

THE DESIGN PARAMETERS OF OE

The structure of this guidebook is based on the five design parameters of organizational engineering, shown on the following page. Here we shall take a brief look at each parameter and the reason for its inclusion in the OE approach.

1. Understanding

To influence the way groups work, we must first identify the factors relevant to how they function — that is, we need an effective way to understand group behavior. OE turns to information processing to meet this need because traditional psychological methods, while perhaps useful for understanding personal behavior, have proven inadequate to meet the challenges presented by large groups of interacting individuals. In its reliance on information processing, OE gains the insight required to meet those

✦ **For more, see Chapter I**

➡ ORGANIZATIONAL ENGINEERING DESIGN PARAMETERS

1. UNDERSTANDING

Systematically identify the factors relevant to the functioning of groups.

2. MEASUREMENT

Create a tool with which the factors identified can be measured accurately.

3. PREDICTION

Show how group behavior can be reliably predicted.

4. GUIDANCE

Provide tools that allow group behavioral changes without requiring individual members to change their values, beliefs, or behavioral preferences.

5. MATERIALITY

Show that the results of this effort will have a material impact on the issue being addressed.

challenges *and* eliminates the need for psychological variables. In the guidebook's chapter on understanding, you will find out more about this important design parameter, including how predicable behaviors can be derived from information-processing choices.

2. Measurement

Understanding is highly useful and often treated as the end-goal in academically based endeavors. In organizational engineering, however, it is simply the start of a process—the first parameter of an overall design.

OE pursues understanding in order to *create measurements* for gauging the factors disclosed by understanding. Crude measurements such as "high-medium-low" yield crude results. Inexact measurements such as "on a scale of 1 to 10" offer only a modest improvement, since we cannot be sure that 5 is half as much as 10; the best we can do is say that 5 is less than 10—just how much less is anybody's

✦ **For more, see Chapter 2**

guess. In the guidebook's chapter on measurement, you will be introduced to the OE method for accurately gauging human preferences.

3. Prediction

Again, whereas many disciplines in the arena of human behavior would stop at this point, organizational engineering goes beyond. It pursues measurement to find a position from which it can *predict outcomes*. Just "explaining" past behavior is insufficient, as the past cannot be changed. Also, the prediction must give us enough time

✦ **For more, see Chapters 3 & 4**

to prepare for the outcome so we can actively influence it; a forecast that precedes an event by only a few min-

utes would be operationally useless. Such issues will
be taken up in two chapters, one focused on individual
behavior and the other on group behavior.

4. Guidance

Once we have forecast an outcome, we need to make
structural adjustments which will alter that outcome in
positive ways. Structural adjustments are group-based
"tools" that change group behavior in a predictable
fashion. With these tools, we can provide groups with
the *guidance* so essential to goal attainment. As the adjustments are group-based,
they do not require personal
changes from group members.
This feature helps OE avoid
the high cost, long delays, and basic uncertainty associated with interventions on an individual level. In this
book, you will learn about two forms of guidance: one
with semi-fixed initiatives and the other with flexible
initiatives.

✦ **For more, see Chapters 5 & 6**

5. Materiality

Finally, OE's engineering orientation requires that
guidance have significant, *material* consequences. We
can make minor improvements in
limited dimensions by using almost any method; but with OE,
our contribution must have a tan-
gible, visible effect on the issue being addressed. This
parameter is covered in the guidebook's last chapter.

✦ **For more, see Chapter 7**

The design parameters of organizational engineering are rigorous, but the tools offered by OE are readily accessible. When we use them, measurement replaces guesswork, solid theory supersedes intuition, and accurate prediction supplants the crossed fingers of hope. As you will see in the following chapters, OE's overall framework demystifies organizational design and moves the human organization a step closer to becoming a process that can be understood and used by everyone for the good of all.

Chapter 1

UNDERSTANDING
THE BASICS OF INFORMATION PROCESSING

IN ORGANIZATIONAL ENGINEERING, our understanding of group behavior is based on the information-processing model shown below. This model gives us a simple but sturdy foundation for measuring, predicting, and guiding group behavior in a way that leads to significant,

DEFINITION REVIEW
➡ **UNDERSTANDING**
Systematically identify the factors relevant to the functioning of groups

positive results. In theory, the model is applicable to any group or individual; but in practice, it is best used with groups. Let's take a closer look.

Figure 1. The Information-Processing Model

THE VALIDITY OF THE MODEL

Our ability to process information is so basic to how we function in the world that most of us seldom think about it. We receive informational input, process that input, and convert it into output almost as naturally as we breathe. Usually, only when our ability is challenged — perhaps the processing requires effort (such as when we learn a complex task), or the input strikes us as particularly important (such as when we must make a weighty decision) — do we become more conscious of ourselves as "information processors."

Anyone who doubts that information processing plays a crucial role in how we function should consider what it would be like to encounter a being who lacked one or more of the information-processing components.

➡ *If unable to receive our input,* the being would seem more like an object than a living entity. We would get no response from it, regardless of how we treated it. We could manipulate it in many ways, but only the laws of physics would determine the results. An entity that does not react to information input beyond that required by physics (i.e., it moves when pushed) would force us to conclude that the being is not an intelligent life form.

➡ *If unable to process our input,* the being might be seen as a kind of pipe. Input goes in at one end and comes out of the other without being transformed in any way. To be considered "intelligent," choices must be made and mere transmission that makes no choices beyond those required by the laws of physics does not qualify. Evaluating such an entity would probably result in our becoming convinced that whatever the being was, it lacked the programming or natural intelligence to work with our input.

➡ *If unable to produce an output,* again, the being might seem like a mere object or a malfunctioning machine. The entity might accept our input but never demonstrate that anything has happened. At best, we may get a signal that indicates the start of processing, and waste our time waiting for an output that will never come. In the end, we wouldn't know what to think about the being. Even if we decided it was a life form, there would be no way of our telling whether it was an intelligent one or not.

As you can see from the above, if we could not process information, we would be unable to function as vital, intelligent beings. We would have no connection to the world around us—and would have no source of knowledge, either practical or conceptual, and no way of contributing to the expansion of knowledge.

The information-processing model, however simple it may appear, thus represents a process of great consequence that we, as functioning human beings, engage in on a continual basis.

FROM PROCESS TO UNDERSTANDING

To better appreciate the complexities of information processing, imagine what the world would be like if everyone processed input in exactly the same way. Behavior would be so predictable, that we would have no need to understand it. Since our "programming" would be identical, there would be no diversity of ideas or opinions; given the same problem (input), everyone would arrive at the same solution (output). Group dynamics would be reduced to group mechanics, in a world of dull agreement.

Now imagine the opposite—a world in which everyone processed input in *entirely* diverse ways. Behavior would be so unpredictable, we would have no common ground for understanding. Given the same problem, everyone would arrive at a different solution. In many ways, agreement about anything would be an impossibility. Such a world is difficult for us to imagine, for it defies our sense of natural law. However highly we prize our unique perspectives as individuals, we recognize in ourselves common operational constructs, both mental and physical, that allow us to relate to one another and help us define what it means to be human.

Clearly, there are factors at work in how we process information that support variances—different outputs for similar input—within a limited range of possibilities. And since an individual is not necessarily confined to producing one specific output for the same input—for instance, someone can come up with multiple solutions to a problem—choice must be a factor in the process.

If we keep to the framework of our processing model, and consider the nature of input and output in light of human limitations and options, three major factors become evident:

1. **The need to filter input.** There are natural limits to how much information we can adequately process at any one time; therefore, we must filter input by deciding what to focus on. This involves organizing, evaluating, and selecting input.

2. **The need to choose a *method* of filtering.** To decide what information we will process, we must draw on some kind of method for sorting out and selecting input, even if that method consists of approaching information in an unsystematic way.

3. **The need to choose a *mode* of response for output.** Although output can vary immensely in its details, there are only so many ways we can express (or deliver) output. Again, we must make a decision: what mode of response we will use.

In the next few pages, we will explore the meaning of these three factors on a practical level, and see how processing links between method and mode result in predictable behavior. We will consider the relevance of method and mode to group performance, and then the place of OE endeavors in relation to traditional psychological approaches.

Information Overload: Filtering Input

Whatever our environment at any given moment, it contains such an abundance of information that our "processing box," though enormous, cannot handle all of it. This is why we screen input, filtering information and deciding what is important—a mental activity so quick and automatic that most of the time we are hardly conscious of performing it.

For example, pause for a couple of minutes and "take in" your immediate surroundings; let your attention wander, focusing and refocusing, and see how much information you can gather. When the time is up, look at the list below, which gives you just a *small* sample of a typical room's informational content.

SAMPLE INPUT: A COMMON ROOM

✦ **LIGHT**
Color
Direction
Diffusion
Ambience

✦ **AIR**
Humidity
Quality
Electrical
  Charge
Oxygen Content
Movement
Pressure
Temperature

✦ **FLOOR**
Color
Covering
Texture
Cleanliness
Level
Firmness

✦ **CEILING**
Color
Texture
Trim
Material
Attachments
Height

✦ **WALLS**
Color
Attachments
Texture
Size
Contour
Angularity
Windows
Doors
Niches
Trim
Solidity
Workmanship
Strength
Flaws

Figure 2. Information Filtering

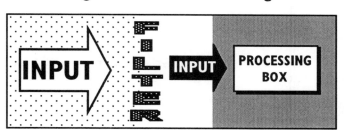

Were you consciously aware of such content before? Most likely in only a general way. Yet some of the information you gathered could have influenced your decision to sit where you are sitting as you read this guidebook! And if it *was* an influence, then for some reason you decided that *that* combination of input was more important to you than another. How did you do that without even realizing it?

The importance of filtering input increases as the issues confronting us, with their active demands on decision making, become more encompassing. And from an information-processing viewpoint, even a relatively simple task common to organizational life—supplying the donuts for an early-morning meeting—has its demands, requiring us to make a surprisingly large number of decisions. Those decisions might include:

- Where to buy the donuts—specialty store, bakery, or supermarket?

- How many to buy—two dozen or three?

- When to buy them—the night before or on the way to work?

- What kind to buy—jelly, frosted, glazed, plain, or other?

- Whether they are fresh—day-old or newly turned out?

- How to carry them to the office—in a box or bag?

- How to display them at the meeting—on paper plates or a plastic tray?

- Where to store them before the meeting—in a back office where no one will nibble at them?

Of course, many of the issues we must deal with on a routine basis require a higher level of decision making than this. Yet we effortlessly make many thousands of such decisions each and every day, automatically filtering out irrelevant input and focusing on what is important. How do we do that?

If we extend our horizon a bit, we might notice that other people make different decisions even when faced with the same issues and operating within roughly the same information environment. Why isn't their way of dealing with those issues the same as ours? Why don't they think like we do?

Filtering Input: METHOD

In answering such questions, most behaviorists would claim there are psychological factors at play. But organi-

Figure 3. The Method Continuum

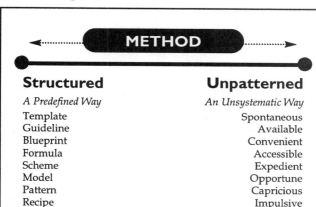

Structured	Unpatterned
A Predefined Way	*An Unsystematic Way*
Template	Spontaneous
Guideline	Available
Blueprint	Convenient
Formula	Accessible
Scheme	Expedient
Model	Opportune
Pattern	Capricious
Recipe	Impulsive
Map	Erratic

zational engineers offer a simpler, clearer answer. People have different, equally legitimate strategies for sorting out the overwhelming amount of information available to them and deciding what to use. Without such strategies, we would spend hours making the simplest choices. It would be like going to a library for a book and having to consider every book before selecting one.

Method is a common denominator among the various strategies we use. As shown in Figure 3, it can be understood as a continuum that runs from a structured to an unpatterned way of sorting out and selecting input. By necessity, we employ some form of method whether making simple or complex decisions, and regardless of the specific information available. There may be more dimensions to information selection but the need to elect a point on the method line cannot be denied. This line, when conjoined with output mode, defines much of the variation witnessed in human behavior.

Directing Output: MODE

The information-processing model also requires that a mode of response be selected for our output. Any output that we might possibly issue necessarily falls somewhere on a continuum ranging from thought to action, as depicted in Figure 4. The point chosen on this continuum determines the character of the output.

As is the case with method, there may be other dimensions to output election, but the need to elect a point on

Figure 4. The Mode Continuum

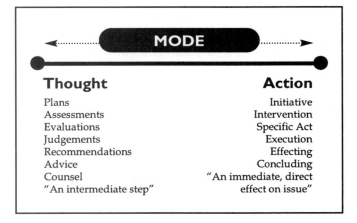

Thought	Action
Plans	Initiative
Assessments	Intervention
Evaluations	Specific Act
Judgements	Execution
Recommendations	Effecting
Advice	Concluding
Counsel	"An immediate, direct
"An intermediate step"	effect on issue"

the mode line is undeniable. Again, in conjunction with method, this line defines much of human behavioral variation.

Linking Method and Mode: Process and Predictability

So far, we have seen that method and mode are essential to information processing:

- Method governs the selection of information flowing into the "processing box."

- Mode governs the nature of the output flowing from it.

Furthermore, because method and mode present human "processors" with options, a person must choose some form of both for information processing to occur. We can think of this necessity as a basic "equation" of processing:

A	➔	**B**	**=**	**C**
CHOICE OF METHOD		**CHOICE OF MODE**		**PROCESSING**

At this point, we are able to show how observable, predictable behaviors "fall out" of, or are derived from, the choice of method and mode.

First, let us consider the choice of *structured method*. By definition, such method involves a disciplined, logical approach to information, with a reliance on some pre-defined way of producing output, whether thought or action. Thus, when structured method is linked to the *thought mode*, a person typically organizes input on the basis of logical connections and detail, with an eye toward some kind of analysis; we can expect this person to take the time necessary to ensure output "makes sense." When structure is linked to the *action mode*, we can anticipate the sort of behaviors shown in Figure 5.

Now, let us consider the choice of *unpatterned method*. This involves a looser, more spontaneous approach to input, with a reliance on informational "prompts" to output, whether thought or action. When unpatterned strategy is linked to the *thought mode*, a person usually selects input on the basis of immediate situational factors, and sees what the relationships among the input elements suggest; we can expect this person to respond faster than someone taking a structured approach, and should not be surprised if the output has unique qualities. This link's potential for producing novel ideas is illustrated and exploited by the exercise of brainstorming, whose general purpose is to get people working in a freer, more creative way with information —a process that involves dispensing with predetermined "structures."

When the unpatterned is linked to the *action mode,* we can again anticipate quick response. And as we see in Figure 5, the choice of method will result in observable behavioral tendencies. In this case, we can expect a person to react to the situational factors that most immediately present themselves. The particular action will thus depend in part on the information environment, but we

Figure 5. Sample Link to Observable Behaviors

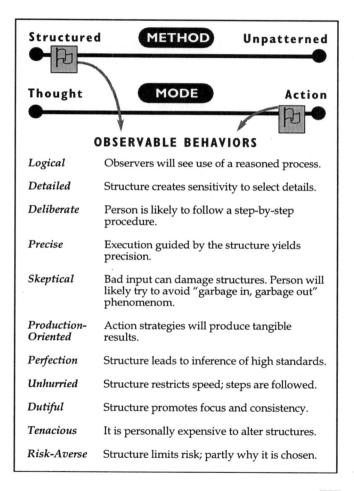

	OBSERVABLE BEHAVIORS
Logical	Observers will see use of a reasoned process.
Detailed	Structure creates sensitivity to select details.
Deliberate	Person is likely to follow a step-by-step procedure.
Precise	Execution guided by the structure yields precision.
Skeptical	Bad input can damage structures. Person will likely try to avoid "garbage in, garbage out" phenomenom.
Production-Oriented	Action strategies will produce tangible results.
Perfection	Structure leads to inference of high standards.
Unhurried	Structure restricts speed; steps are followed.
Dutiful	Structure promotes focus and consistency.
Tenacious	It is personally expensive to alter structures.
Risk-Averse	Structure limits risk; partly why it is chosen.

can expect it to be "in the moment," and to lack a fully reasoned-out procedure. Getting action output delivered to resolve the issue at hand is likely to be a top priority.

Before we move on, it is important to emphasize that the mode of response we select, whether thought or action, is not necessarily determined by method; however, mode *does* reflect the tendencies associated with the ultimately chosen method—this contributes to behavioral predictability. For example, a person who takes a rigorously structured approach to information is unlikely to come up with startling new ideas. We can also infer that the person has chosen this method partly because it yields a high certainty of outcome; thus, it is highly unlikely that any action output will be capricious.

➡ INFORMATION-PROCESSING RECAP

So far we have learned that . . .

— All of us are information processors operating in environments laden with input.

— We need a method for selecting input to process, and a mode of response for delivering output.

— Our choices of method and mode are limited to continuums and linked in processing.

— Out of those choices fall observable, predictable behaviors.

The Relevance to Group Performance

We have taken a close look at the information-processing model and its dimensions of method and mode. Their role as factors relevant to group performance becomes clearer if we consider the following:

- In any group or team situation, people feed one another information in pursuit of common goals; one person's output is another's input, along an ongoing informational chain. At each link in that chain is a chance for reinterpretation, because of the variables necessarily inherent in processing (i.e., method and mode), and so information can become altered enough to affect group performance.

  It follows that if we can find a way to anticipate the method and mode of group members — their "strategic styles" of dealing with information, and the behavior that accompanies those styles — we can plan interventions and other forms of guidance to ensure improved group performance.

- The decision-making situations in which groups must function intensify the importance of the informational chain and strategic styles. All issues rely on these factors for their effective resolution, but the consequence is magnified when dealing with issues of significance.

  If we want improved results from group decision making, then, we need to guide information's flow through that chain, ensuring that the character of the information matches the needs of the issues at hand.

☎ Remember "Telephone"?

Also known as "Gossip," this is a children's circle game in which a message initiated by one player is passed along, person to person and "in secret," until it has gone round. The final player states the message for all to hear; then the first player states the original. The result? Fits of laughter, for the "same" message has somehow turned into two different ones.

Information flow among adults does not escape this natural distortion, a consequence of information-processing variables. However, in organizations, where such flow is crucial to effective decision making and group performance, the results can be and often are far from amusing. They can affect the quality and possibly the very existence of our lives.

In Chapter 2, we will see how it is possible to develop behavioral measurements based on method and mode, for use in determining individual and group strategic styles. OE instruments employ such measurement, and help us get on course to predicting and guiding group behavior.

OE and Its Relationship to Psychology

There is a rule called Occam's Razor, used in both science and philosophy, which dictates that hypotheses be pared down to the minimum, with the simplest explanation set above the rest. Why is the simplest to be preferred? Because it is free of inessentials, which can mislead and result in error. Each distinct factor in an explanation can be seen as an opportunity for error. In seeking what is essential to improving group performance, organizational engineering wields Occam's Razor and in the process cuts away much of psychology that, while significant on an individual level, is unnecessary on a group level.

This does not mean OE ignores the individual, only that its considerations at that level are made in service to understanding, measuring, predicting, and guiding *group* behavior. It does not seek to change individuals in a fundamental way — to "plumb their depths." Consequently, OE can rely on much simpler explanations of behavior than can traditional psychology.

Of course, with this simplicity comes limits. OE does not explain *all* behaviors — just what it needs to explain for its purposes — and so there is a legitimate role for psychology and its particular brand of understanding. In terms of the proper time to use these disciplines, guidelines for the manager are fairly straightforward:

Use . . .

➡ **ORGANIZATIONAL ENGINEERING when the issue concerns group performance or behavior**

➡ **PSYCHOLOGY when the issue concerns a single individual**

There may be cases that require a combination of the two disciplines and their respective tools; but generally, managers should find these guidelines helpful and well worth following.

The astute manager would do well to recognize and exploit the differences between OE and psychology, especially in their instrumentation. Be aware, though, of correlations between the two which may blur distinctions. For example, the Keirsey Temperament Sorter*—a Myers-Briggs type of tool—asks:

> *"Do you tend to look for*
> *(a) the orderly; (b) whatever turns up"*

This is obviously an information-processing question (related to method), revealing a correlation with OE. But other questions depart from the OE arena, such as:

> *"Is it harder for you to*
> *(a) identify with others; (b) utilize others"*

Here we are dealing with purely psychological variables.

Correlations like the one above simply mean there is *a relationship* between psychology and OE; they do not make the two any more the same than we are the same as chimpanzees, with whom we share a 98 percent correlation of DNA. To distinguish between OE elements and psychological ones, remember:

Organizational engineering focuses on information, its processing, and the decisions that accompany processing.

---

*From *Please Understand Me!* David Keirsey and Marilyn Bates, Prometheus Nemesis Book Co.: 1984.

Chapter 2

MEASUREMENT
CREATING THE STANDARD OE TOOL

WE NOW KNOW that the information-processing factors of method and mode are critical to our understanding of group behavior. Organizational engineers develop measurements for these factors, to determine strategic styles of information processing; instruments based on such measurement are then created. In this way, OE equips managers with tools for predicting group behavior, so that guidance can be planned. This chapter will explain why developing a useful measurement is possible, and give you an inside look at how it is done.

> **DEFINITION REVIEW**
>
> ➡ **MEASUREMENT**
> A way of accurately estimating relative magnitudes of selected factors — in this case, method and mode

THE POSSIBILITY OF USEFUL MEASUREMENT

In Chapter 1, we established the following:

- Everyone must make a choice of method and mode in order to process information.

- These factors are limited to continuums and linked in processing.

- Our choice of method and mode has observable, predictable behavioral consequences.

When we review these facts in light of measurement, a question naturally arises. Although the continuums are limited and linked, they still represent a great range of options and behaviors; thus, if people are commonly free to choose from among all the possibilities (i.e., any set of two points along the method and mode lines), how can we develop a measurement that will be useful *before* a choice is made? It seems we are faced with a behavioral "wild card": the arbitrary nature of choice.

The answer to this dilemma is suggested by our experience of other adults, ourselves, and the social relationships that connect us. There are stabilizing forces that strengthen method-mode preferences and, in structured environments like the workplace, actively keep our options within certain ranges. Let's take a closer look.

The Constraints of Freedom

Normally, people are bound by two forces that keep their choice of method and mode within predictable ranges.

1. **Specialization.** By the time we are adults, most of us have learned firsthand that "practice makes perfect." We tend to develop certain skills, use those skills, and thereby increase our proficiency at them. The more proficient we get, the easier use becomes,

Figure 6. Sample Range of Method-Mode Options

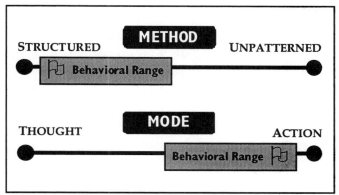

and the more apt we are to draw on those skills and use them as a base for further development. Our strengths, then, tend to guide our choices — and limit them. The behaviors that accompany those choices are part of what "typifies" us to others; they help to shape us as individuals with behavioral patterns that can be anticipated and gauged by others.

It is virtually impossible to avoid some form of specialization in life. Anyone who actively avoids it will eventually become skilled at, and specialized in, mediocrity.

2. **Social constraint.** Social forces also compel us to behave in certain ways, and so limit our operational ranges (one such range is shown in Figure 6). For instance, in organizations others expect us to deliver

a certain character of output (their input), based on what we have delivered in the past; if we do not deliver it, they will act to correct what they view as a dysfunctional condition—a "bad link" in the informational chain that has upset work plans, impeding their progress. Consistency in behavior is a common type of social constraint in any organization, and it keeps all of us within relatively narrow ranges of method and mode selection.

For a demonstration of social constraint and its importance, try out the exercise "Surprise."

Since we can expect to find people functioning within such limits, useful measurement is indeed possible. We will not end up with "scatter graphs" of unrelated behavioral choices, worthless for predicting anything but confusion; but rather, we will find logical, consistence behaviors that we can group into intelligible strategic styles, and on which we can base instrumentation.

CREATING AN OPERATIONAL MEASURE

Our goal is to create a scale that has a *direct, measurable behavioral reference,* that is, an immediate meaning in observable behaviors. We want to be able to observe or otherwise survey behavior later on and find its position on our scale. This will give us a foundation for behavioral prediction.

In working toward our goal, we must remember:

• Method and mode are not discrete components of

EXERCISE: "Surprise"
A Demonstration of Social Constraint

✦ Mentally place yourself within your normal work environment doing your normal activities. Now imagine that you suddenly decide to shift your work approach radically.

— If you are deliberate and thoughtful (use the structured as method, and thought as mode), start ignoring details and taking immediate action (shift to unpatterned action).

— If you are disciplined and production-oriented (use the structured as method, and action as mode), begin offering ideas "off the top of your head" but without suggesting how they could be accomplished (shift to unpatterned thought).

✦ What do you envision as your coworkers' responses to your sudden change? Does it include their telling you to "be yourself"?

Negative reactions to such changes are not malicious. People come to depend on you for a certain kind of output (their input). When you shift behavior, you compromise their ability to perform.

With everyone protecting themselves, a network of social constraint is formed that helps keep people within a certain range of behaviors. No one escapes, be they boss or subordinate.

---

information processing, but linked in processing. Consequently, at some point these links must be incorporated into our scale.

• The continuums of method and mode do not lend themselves to absolute values: we do not measure behavior as we measure a person's height. There is no such thing as "two inches more" thought or "two inches less" action. But we can say that there is a point where the structured ends and the unpatterned begins—likewise in the case of thought and action—and we can assign that point a neutral value (zero). From that point on, the scaling of these elements is based on *behavioral* degree.

• We have come to measurement knowing that our task has been bounded by limited ranges of method and mode; therefore, we must ensure that our scale accommodates such ranges.

The Steps to Measurement

There are four steps to measurement:

1. To begin, we divide our continuums into their four basic elements. This gives us a starting point for measuring each element: the structured, the unpatterned, thought, and action. Such a division is a necessity: it lets us plot a zero point for each element and ensures that each element is given the same weight.

2. We now combine method and mode to incorporate the links between them. The possible combinations, shown in Figure 7, create four new factors, replacing the old method and mode continuums. This brings us to an important level in our measurement development. We have forfeited the distinct categories of method and mode but gained the following:

Figure 7. Measurement—Step 2

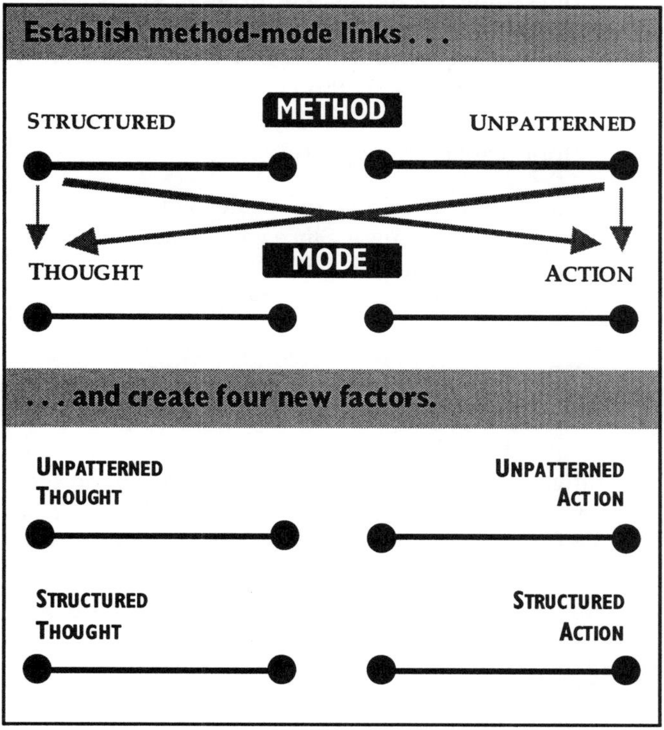

Establish method-mode links . . .

STRUCTURED METHOD UNPATTERNED

THOUGHT MODE ACTION

. . . and create four new factors.

UNPATTERNED
THOUGHT

UNPATTERNED
ACTION

STRUCTURED
THOUGHT

STRUCTURED
ACTION

— A measure *directly* related to human behavior; any point on any line has an immediate mean ing in observable behaviors. Each line is now itself a workable scale of measurement in an overall measurement tool.

— A basis for establishing strategic styles. Our four factors have been implied all along by the links between method and mode; in this step, they are simply made explicit. Because these are the only combinations of method and mode possible, we can legitimately consider them representative of four distinct strategic styles.

3. Next, we must see how our scales will accommodate behavioral ranges. Since we are dealing with a combination of method and mode, we should have no problem translating those ranges.

   Figure 8 shows a sample translation for two ranges: in one, unpatterned method is the extreme; in the other, thought mode is the extreme. The process is simple. We take the maximum degrees of the two ranges and locate their combined position on the new "unpatterned thought" scale. Since the scale begins at zero, everything between the end of the flag (x) range and zero must also be behaviorally accessible. The same process is repeated for the other three lines.

   The result is a set of four behavioral ranges likely to be exhibited by the person who was measured. These ranges suggest where we should place "tick marks" indicating degrees of behavior.

4. Finally, we want to adjust the structure of our tool; right now, the relationships between the scales are difficult to gauge and measurement is too flat to be

Figure 8. Measurement—Step 3

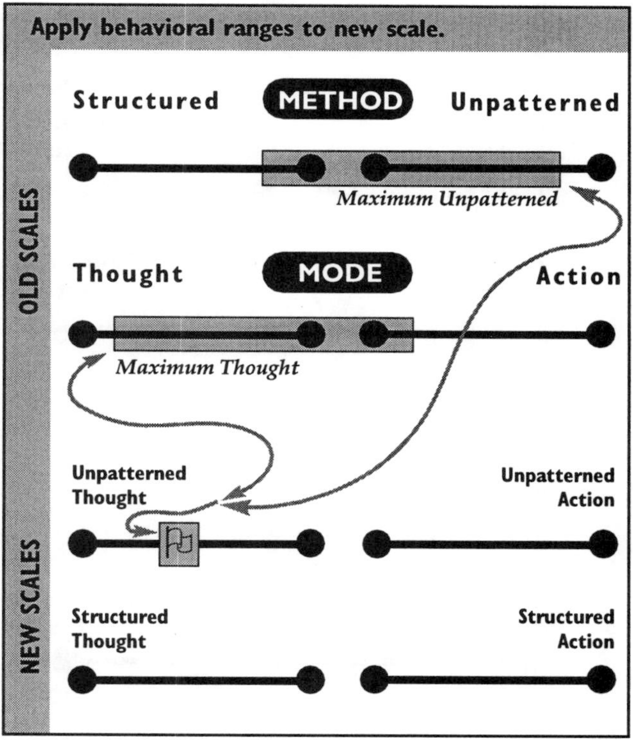

Apply behavioral ranges to new scale.

OLD SCALES

Structured — **METHOD** — Unpatterned

Maximum Unpatterned

Thought — **MODE** — Action

Maximum Thought

NEW SCALES

Unpatterned Thought

Unpatterned Action

Structured Thought

Structured Action

readily understood. We need to tighten up our tool so it will give us a quick and easy "picture" of behavior.

Figure 9. Measurement—Step 4

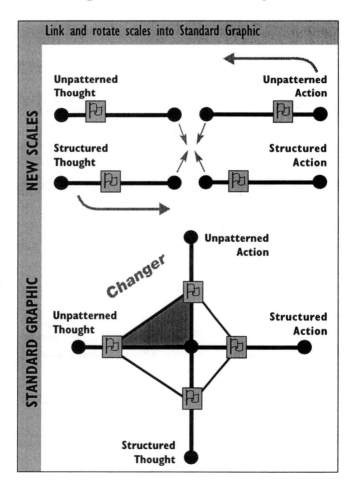

To accomplish this, we merely connect all scales at their zero point and rotate two of them into a perpendicular position, as shown in Figure 9. We now have a vertical axis and a horizontal one: a "standard graphic" that will serve us well. Plotting on these scales will now produce a visible profile of behavior; we have only to connect our flags (x's) across scales.

Remember, the hub of our tool will always represent the zero point for all scales, from which we measure *outward* in degrees of magnitude.

We now have a measuring tool—called the Standard Graphic—that is 100 percent related to specific behaviors and that depicts relatively stable estimates of future behaviors. There are two elements about this tool worth noting.

- The repositioning of the scales was not arbitrary. By moving them the way we did, we created a circle of four variables whose progression carries some common link of origin. For example, the area labeled "Changer" in Figure 9 spans two axes that share unpatterned method but differ on mode, with one favoring thought and the other action. The quadrant we create in linking the points of degree on those axes gives us a combined measurement—something that will prove especially useful when we need to predict the behaviors of people who are not committed to a particular strategic style.

- The preservation of the zero point ensures that we

do not "misread" the relationships between oppo-
sitely placed axes (or scales). The opposite ends of
the same axis are *not* negatives of each other; their
original relationship was set by their functionality
as limited options in information processing, not
by diametrical opposition in meaning or in value.
For example, a person approaching an issue seeking a high certainty of tangible results using structured action as a vehicle cannot simultaneously
employ unpatterned thought. The unpatterned
element comprises certainty and the focus of energy
on "thought" limits tangibility of outcome. Such an
effort would be self-cancelling. Humans have fig-
ured this out and so do not typically engage in it.

The latter point has significant implications for the attributes we attach to the styles. It discourages the attribution of value to styles, notably the depreciation of one
style by the declared worth of another. Such imbalance
can subvert the very purpose of measurement. We cannot
guide groups effectively if some members feel their styles
are "bad" and so carry less weight. As we know from the
origins of the styles, "good" and "bad" have nothing to
do with information processing: thought is not intrinsically better or worse than action; the structured is not
intrinsically better or worse than the unpatterned.

This problem is a common stumbling block in instrumentation. For example, we find it in the Myers-Briggs diagnostic, where "introvert" and "extrovert" exist on oppo-

site ends of the same scale. Although they were never intended to have positive or negative connotations, their blank opposition invites attribution: if one is declared good, the other "must" be bad. Practitioners argue that introversion and extroversion are devoid of judgmental meaning. But ask the clients of these practitioners their view and you will find strong positive and negative connotations have indeed become attached. This condition diminishes the value of the instrumentation.

Fortunately, we have structured our Standard Graphic along design lines that minimize this effect. Declaring that one axis is "good" does not mean another is "bad" any more than declaring that a hammer is "good" means a screwdriver is "bad." They are simply different things. This design feature will come into play when we discuss the labeling-theory concerns that typically arise with any kind of instrument that classifies people.

NAMING THE STRATEGIC STYLES

The Standard Graphic is now operationally serviceable but still lacks one thing: a practical nomenclature for the styles it will be used to measure. We need to rename our axes so we can distinguish them more clearly and communicate the results of measurement as easily as possible. Of course, since OE is concerned with the integrity of what it builds, these names should not be arbitrary.

To meet this need, OE looks at the two main facets of each style:

Figure 10. Naming the Strategic Styles

NAME	METHOD	MODE
Reactive Stimulator	**Unpatterned**	**Action**

- "Reactive" describes a style inclined to pay attention to immediate factors.
- "Stimulator" describes a tendency to act quickly on those factors.

Logical Processor	**Structured**	**Action**

- "Logical" describes an approach that favors disciplined, sequential reasoning methods.
- "Processor" speaks to the methodical application of action to the issue at hand.

Hypothetical Analyzer	**Structured**	**Thought**

- "Hypothetical" refers to the tendency to consider situations that might arise.
- "Analyzer" addresses the way the issue at hand is likely to be resolved.

Relational Innovator	**Unpatterned**	**Thought**

- "Relational" describes a way of linking unpatterned elements.
- "Innovator" speaks to the likely outcome of unique and novel approaches.

1. "How" an issue is approached
2. "What" the outcome is likely to be

The pair of terms used to name the axes reflects method and mode, the factors at the very core of our measuring tool. The most notable characteristics of each is used to determine the style name. Figure 10 shows the set of strategic styles and their descriptions.

This nomenclature has two important benefits:

• First, no matter which style we fall into, we are not going to feel overly excited or terribly insulted by its name. This prevents unwanted connotations from attaching to the styles: their names tend to repel such valuation, keeping things fairly neutral.

• Second, the names are perfect prompts for initialization; indeed, in practice, people simply refer to themselves and others as, say, an "HA" or "RI." This further minimizes the chance of their attaching negative connotations to the styles. Concerns over labeling are reduced, and, as a bonus, communication is expedited by the verbal "shortcuts."

Large-scale field experience ($n > 10,000$) confirms that this naming strategy works as expected. The names are used without hesitation and their meaning is grasped without ambiguity. They fit the engineering model.

The Behavioral Markers of Measurement

We now have a measuring tool that directly references behavior, presents strategic styles, and helps ensure that no one will be affected adversely by its use. We do not, however, have specific behavioral referents that allow us to plot individual or group style profiles on our tool. Those — the "tick" marks that reference behaviors — are provided by OE instrumentation.

Essentially, the Strategic Style Instrument requires a person to "Trade-Off" behavioral preferences associated with each of the four styles. The proportion of times the person elects a particular style can be seen as an index of the strength of that preference. For example, choosing the Hypothetical Analyzer Response 75 percent of the time gives us a ratio measure of that preference relative to the other selections available. Unlike psychological tools, OE has unit measures — "tick marks" that stay in the same place wherever applied.

OE "rulers" come in various forms and can be chosen to suit the needs of the user. However, all have common characteristics. First, all carry the Certification of the Organizational Engineering Institute, Inc., of Ann Arbor, Michigan. This means they have been statistically checked against a large database that was created as the discipline was developed. Instruments without this certification cannot be depended upon.

Second, all of them "trade off" behavioral characteristics

of each of the strategic styles. The content and sequence of items allow the respondent to choose from four equally legitimate behavioral approaches, each of which correspond to a particular style. The resultant scores reliably describe the respondent's underlying ranges of method and mode, and the relative proportion of choices can be transferred to the Standard Graphic.

To receive a free copy of **DecideX**—a certified organizational engineering instrument — call 800-860-1361, or write to HRD Press, Inc., 22 Amherst, MA, 01002-9709.

At this point, we have outlined the basic theory underlying organizational engineering—that behaviors are generated by information-processing choices. We have also developed a measurement tool for gauging the strategic styles associated with those choices. Now it is time to see how we can apply this material to the accurate prediction of individual and group behavior.

Chapter 3

PREDICTING INDIVIDUAL BEHAVIOR

PREDICTING THE BEHAVIOR OF INDIVIDUALS is important to organizational engineering for a simple reason: groups are composed of individual members, and the strategic styles of those members will contribute to the overall style of the group. In working to-

DEFINITION REVIEW

➡ **PREDICTION**
  Show how group behavior
  can be reliably predicted

ward prediction, we must understand that OE does not try to forecast isolated behaviors—for example, how someone will make one particular decision or another. Working with such a narrow focus would strain the limits of predictability and yield little information, if any, about the larger outcomes with which we are concerned. It would be analogous to a casino trying to predict a gambler's win or loss on one throw of the die, in order to project its daily wins or losses. Casinos rely on statistical probabilities; we rely on strategic styles and their probable effect on *a stream* or *sequence of decisions* made by an individual or a group.

Essentially, this is only common sense. It is rare when one decision alone results in a highly consequential outcome.

Deciding to pursue a college education is a single, important decision. But the nature of the outcome — the value of the degree to be gained — will be determined by tens of thousands of decisions, from which classes to elect to whether to cut class on a certain day. It is the nature of the decision sequence that is and should be the focus of organizational engineering.

STRATEGIC PROFILES AND THEIR USE

As we saw in Chapter 2, the Standard Graphic presents four strategic styles whose scales are linked at the central "zero" point. When someone's behavior is plotted on the graphic, and measurement is linked, we receive a picture (technically, a quadrilateral) of the response range within which the person is typically confined. We call this picture a *strategic profile,* and can expect a person's usual behavior to fall somewhere within its boundaries. In Figure 11, the strategic-profile area has now been labeled, with new style names applied to the axes.

Does this profile mean that only behaviors within its boundaries are possible? Of course not. If a particular issue clearly calls for a response outside a person's preferred boundaries, the person will probably elect that response. For example, if you notice a child drowning, it is unlikely you will pause to devise a creative way of saving the child or begin planning the perfect rescue. You will most likely react without hesitation, diving in or grabbing whatever is at hand — the Reactive Stimulator approach. The situation clearly calls for it.

Figure 11. Sample Strategic Profile

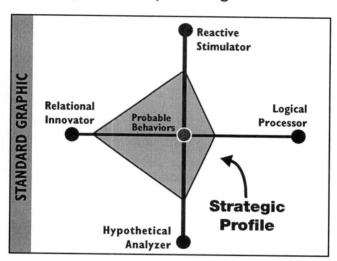

However, most issues that confront us do not have a clearly defined "optimal" approach. For example, let's say a competitor introduces a new product that seems targeted directly at your firm's "bread and butter" offering. What is the ideal response?

- Should you take the time to analyze their product, thereby giving them an increased opportunity to gain a foothold?

- Should you quickly increase advertising, even though money will be wasted if the competitor's product fails on its own?

- Should you move to jump the competitor with your own innovative product at the risk that it may fall flat?

- Should you just keep doing what you are doing, and see what happens?

The board of directors meets in one hour and will be looking for your advice. *What is your decision?*

Clearly, this kind of situation has no "right" answer. A legitimate case can be made for all of the options. It is likely that your decision will follow the behavioral preferences described by your strategic profile. A self-examination will likely reveal that most of the decisions you make are of this character. There is usually no "right" time to buy a car, no "right" restaurant to have dinner at tonight, and no "right" way to prioritize the stack of work sitting on your desk.

Determining Probable Response

Two important factors influence predictability of response:

1. Strength of Style
2. Style Patterns

Strength of Style

People usually employ all four strategic styles to some degree. The strength of these styles can be graphed in rank order, as shown in Figure 12. On a decision-by-decision basis, this style distribution provides a measure of

Figure 12. Distribution of Style Preferences

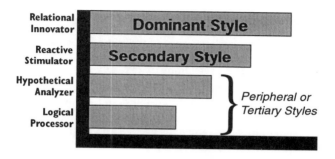

the likelihood that a particular style will be used. For example, the sample graph in Figure 12 tells us that the Relational Innovator (RI) strategy would likely be used for making any particular decision; Reactive Stimulator (RS) would the next most likely choice. This graph is based on the sample strategic profile presented earlier in Figure 11.

Most people depend on strategic styles to help coordinate their actions with others. Often coordination involves issues requiring timely decision making, with a focus on what people are likely to contribute to those issues. Contributions can vary within similar styles, but the behavioral orientations attached to the styles give each style a particular character, and particular strengths when it comes to contribution. The greater the degree of a style dominance in someone's profile, the stronger the style will be, and the more likely that its orientations will be

Figure 13. Summary of Strategic Styles

REACTIVE STIMULATOR (RS)

The pure RS is an action-oriented individual. RSs have a tendency to react immediately. They are highly focused on the task at hand and seek immediate results.

The strength of the RS is the ability to act quickly and to be comfortable in making decisions with minimal information and detail. This can be especially valuable in situations where an immediate remedy is needed and the means by which the remedy is accomplished is of secondary concern. Emergency room staffs must often deal with such situations and usually have a high RS component.

LOGICAL PROCESSOR (LP)

The LP is the "bulldog" of the four styles. LPs are logical, methodical, and not easily deterred. They are naturally detail-oriented people who prefer assignments that are clear and precise, with well-defined expectations.

The strength of the LP is the ability to define and execute programs, methodologies, and techniques in a disciplined fashion. Precision, certainty, and an inclination toward action characterizes this strategic posture. Surgeons and scientists often have a high LP component.

HYPOTHETICAL ANALYZER (HA)

The HA is a problem solver. Issues are analyzed carefully and pondered from many viewpoints. HAs typically enjoy complexity and the challenge of solving difficult problems. They are cautious and proceed carefully. Their major focus is on planning and assessment. They usually prefer to leave the actual execution of plans to others.

The strength of the HA style is the ability to analyze and assess complicated problems and situations. People with this style are typically able to communicate the results of their study quite effectively. They are particularly well suited to assessing options and creating plans on subjects of material magnitude and complexity. Many judges, teachers, and professors have HA as a dominant style.

RELATIONAL INNOVATOR (RI)

The pure RI deals in ideas and sees things in "big picture" terms. Relationships between divergent ideas and situations are quickly identified. RIs are often innovators and like to explore different ways of doing things. Concepts, ideas, and innovations are quickly integrated into coherent theories and systems.

The strength of the RI style is the ability to focus on new and varied ways of accomplishing things. This style is characterized by minimal attention to detail and the ability to rapidly generate new, often unusual ways of addressing a situation. Inventors and entrepreneurs typically have a strong RI component.

---

exhibited in a person's behavior. Figure 13 summarizes these orientations.

Strategic Patterns

If we are interested in the characterization of someone's style preferences over a sequence of decisions, the preferred approach is to look at the strategic patterns in the person's profile. Strategic patterns are combinations of adjacent styles, with patterns estimated by comparing the profile areas of the quadrants.

Figure 14. Sample Dominant Pattern: Changer

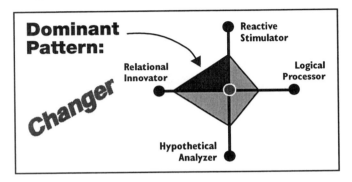

In Figure 14, the profile area in the RI-RS quadrant is larger than the area in any other quadrant. It indicates the likelihood that the behavior patterns common to the RI and RS styles will be exhibited over time. This, in turn, will influence judgment of the behavioral "personality" of the individual in question. Figure 15 summarizes the four possible strategic patterns indicated by strategic profiles.

The ability to predict individual behavior over a series of decisions should now be apparent. The stronger the commitment to a strategic style, the more likely it is that the committed person will exhibit behaviors consistent with that style. The stronger the pattern, the more likely it is that the pattern will come to typify that person's overall behavior.

Figure 15. Summary of Strategic Patterns

PERFORMER: **Combines the RS and LP styles**

This pattern tends to be task-specific, action-oriented, and focused on tangible achievement. Performers tend to take a relatively short-range perspective on situations and are able to make quick decisions.

CONSERVATOR: **Combines the LP and HA styles**

This pattern is typified by a careful, detail-oriented approach and a tendency towards skepticism when new situations are at hand. Long preparation time and careful execution usually result in consistent quality of output.

PERFECTER: **Combines the HA and RI styles**

This pattern generates and values new ideas, but tends to express them only after they have been "perfected" by exhaustive consideration of risk, reward, and contingencies. Because the pattern references both innovation and assessment, it is often found in good advisors.

CHANGER: **Combines the RI and RS styles**

This pattern tends to generate new ideas quickly and to begin implementing them immediately. Changers typically rely on an experimental strategy, rather than planning and analysis, to evaluate the worth of a particular initiative. They are usually averse to detail, rapid in response, and innovative in approach.

We now know how style profiles can help us predict behavior. However, some profiles can complicate this predictability. We will look at them next.

Problematic Profiles

In general, there are two kinds of style profiles that make prediction difficult:

> 1. Split Strategic Style
> 2. Balanced Strategic Style

Split Strategic Style

"Split style" is a condition where a person's primary and secondary strategic styles lie at opposite ends of the same axis; that is, the primary and secondary styles differ in both method and mode.

Figure 16 illustrates an example of a split style. It suggests that someone with this style might seem a little "off-center" to an outside observer. In one situation, the person might avoid detail, rapidly generating new ideas and reaching decisions without hesitation. In another situation, perhaps immediately following the first, he or she might pursue detail to extreme lengths, tending toward well-tested solutions and approaching decisions with caution. The result? A very perplexed observer.

Does this mean prediction is impossible? No, because style patterns will still be apparent. If we look again at Figure 16, we see a dominant pattern of Perfecter. Thus,

Figure 16. Sample Split-Style Profile

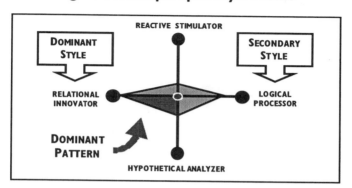

when viewing this person's performance over time, the observer is likely to conclude this is someone who more often than not focuses on carefully evaluating and examining new ideas, with a high concern for presenting organized and well thought out plans. The person remains difficult to predict, but the severity of the observer's judgment may be mitigated.

A more severe case of split style is the needle split style, exemplified in Figure 17, which follows. Here the primary and secondary styles lie on opposite ends of the same axis, but there is no dominant strategic pattern. This type of person is truly difficult to characterize in both the short and the long term.

It should be pointed out that these contradictory tendencies are not a problem for the individuals who have them.

Figure 17. Sample "Needle" Split Style

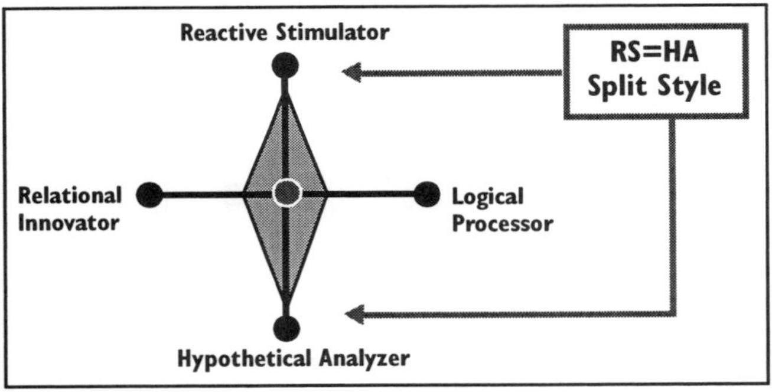

For any given decision they must make, these people "know" which option is to be preferred; effectively, they have built in a "switch" that tells them which to choose. The strategic profile has been successful in getting them to where they are, and there is nothing to fix. It simply works. Common split-style "switches" are presented in Figure 18.

While the "switching" mechanism is interesting, it is really not unusual. People switch among primary, secondary, and tertiary strategic styles all of the time. What makes the split style significant is that the behaviors are contradictory in character and seem to happen arbitrarily. This, in turn, makes coordination with other people difficult.

Figure 18. Common Split-Style Switches

To navigate between divergent styles, individuals often rely on the following "switch" mechanisms:

LOCATION: Example: *using RI at home and LP in the workplace.*

CONSEQUENCE: Example: *using RS for low-consequence decisions and HA for high-exposure choices.*

PHYSICAL: Example: *using HA when fresh and alert, and RS when tired or stressed.*

SOCIAL: Example: *using LP when few people are present, and RI when many people are involved.*

There is no need for the individuals with the split style to change or even to identify the switch. The strategic posture works for them—it got them where they are. It is not even important that others "discover" the switch. It is only important that they be able to anticipate the character of response. The most usual way this can be accomplished is through a signaling mechanism.

For example, an OE analysis was conducted for a large fabric manufacturer in the Southeast. The clients included a general manager, his immediate staff, and the staffs of two plants that reported to him. It turned out that the general manager had a marked RS–HA split style.

The result of the individual analysis was reviewed with the general manager. He had been unaware of his contradictory tendencies but, during the review session, readily agreed that he possessed them. The in-house consultant conducting the session then pointed out that the manager's strategic posture was generating added overhead on the part of people who worked with him.

The general manager's staff and the people at the plant recognized his markedly divergent preferences but, of course, could not predict them. Their solution was to invest in detailed and thorough preparation that he would find appropriate if in his HA posture. If it turned out that he was in his RS mode, they could always "back down" to the quick response, the minimal detail posture favored by that style. The reverse was not possible, for if they prepared for his RS style election, the detail would not be available.

The consultant pointed out the net result to the general manager—that the staffs were investing effort and money for detailed preparation, even when issues might not warrant such investment. The manager's response was sudden and a bit humorous. He had a flag-holder put up outside his office and got two flags of different colors: one indicated he was using his RS style; the other indicated he was currently favoring his HA.

The general manager also addressed this subject in the debriefing sessions for the entire group. He told them that he would signal his needs as assignments were given; if he forgot, the group should ask him about his needs before they invested work and money in an issue.

This individual used the most common remedy for addressing split-style issues — a signaling mechanism to explicitly tell people what he expected. His strategy was a bit more thorough than most, however, as he also set up a fail-safe mechanism, giving his staff permission to inquire about his needs if he forgot to signal them. A check with the consultant confirmed that the process was still working two years after the intervention.

The strategy for split-style signaling is straightforward:

1. If you are the superior, recognize that you may be in situations that could be frustrating to your staff and misdirect them. Signal your needs on an issue-by-issue basis.

2. If you are a subordinate, recognize that coworkers may not be able to fully coordinate their efforts with yours. You might be able to improve your performance and theirs by adopting a mutually acceptable signaling strategy.

A review of an OE development database ($n>8000$) indicates that up to 13 percent of the population examined have split styles. If restricted to split styles of pronounced magnitudes, the percentage drops to about 6 percent. In either case, the magnitude is sufficient to warrant systematic attention. In providing that attention, we might be wise to remember that split style can also be used to an

Figure 19. Balanced Strategic Profile

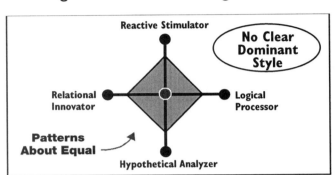

advantage: people using it are often great "switch hitters" in addressing group issues.

While split styles are the most dramatic causes for individual unpredictability, there is another profile that can introduce coordination issues as well: balanced strategic styles.

Balanced Strategic Style

Strategic profiles sometimes show equal measurement in all four quadrants of the Standard Graphic. When that occurs, the profile is described as "balanced." The ambiguity inherent in this sort of style, illustrated in Figure 19, is apparent. There is no consistent direction that might be predicted by either pattern or style preference. Consequently, balanced styles are as difficult to predict as split styles.

A case example of the operational difficulties of a balanced style is found in the experience of a senior-level professional working for a major retailer. She reported that her position involved supporting other members of the staff in pursuit of group objectives. She said that she had been continually surprised when her work contribution did not meet a welcome reception from the people requesting her services. The issue became clear after she saw her strategic profile. Whereas she had been attributing the difficulty to the quality of the staff, she now saw it as a mismatch of expectations. The solution was simple; she said, "I am now asking people who come in exactly what they are expecting in return." Her profile equips her to match any likely expectation. She is a great "utility infielder."

STRATEGIC PROFILE CHANGES

Strategic profiles are not necessarily permanent. They are merely strategies that people use to navigate within their environments. If these strategies begin to yield consistently unsatisfactory results, an individual will normally alter his or her approach. Figure 20, following, illustrates a transition of this type.

The author has witnessed several individuals' self-initiated, purposeful style transitions. A complete profile transition appears to take about 18 months on average. However, more modest transitions have occurred in about six months. The one constant in all of these changes is that the transition is not easy.

Figure 20. Strategic-Style Transition

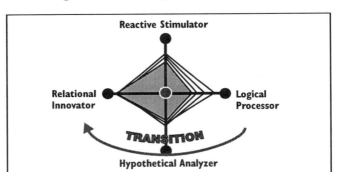

Such transitions are generally difficult because the strategic profile is an ongoing behavioral influence, operating in all of the environments of a person's life. Someone does not shift his or her behavioral "personality" on the drive home from work. This stability is a consequence of specialization, discussed in Chapter 2.

Sample environments in which strategic styles tend to remain constant include:

- **Work** — Within the work group, among people contacted in the course of business, and so forth

- **Family** — Spouse, children, parents, extended family members

- **Friends** — Neighbors, professional affiliations, casual acquaintances, close friends, and so on

- **Interests** — Political, social, educational, religious, recreational, and so on

Individuals will typically choose a strategic style profile that "works" in all of the environments in which they participate.

Transition Through Environmental Conditioning: Two Examples

To see what is involved in actually changing a person's style profile, we can turn to the example of medical training. Surgeons must be precise, careful, methodical, detail-oriented, fully knowledgeable, and otherwise true to the qualities of a Logical Processor. As we can assume people enter medical school with a variety of strategic profiles, how do schools ensure that students initially without the LP style acquire it in training?

The answer is, mainly by controlling their environment. The "book learning" phase lays the groundwork by building a rationale for the style's use. Students become immersed in a curriculum that leaves no time for family or friends, and so are effectively isolated in an environment that conditions them to prefer LP behaviors. For instance, on rounds students are closely questioned about the current status of each patient visited. Errors are put on full display in front of their peers. It does not take long for a student to figure out that the LP strategy is the one that means survival.

Also, as skill in the style is acquired, students begin to see its value, enjoying the satisfaction of disciplined precision and the style's high certainty of outcome. The full process, through residency, takes from six to nine years.

Military training is another, simpler example. The military needs people who understand and appreciate the need for structure and action-oriented discipline. To ensure a certain baseline level of the LP style, they separate recruits from all other environments during basic training. For 12 weeks the recruit is confined to a carefully structured environment, under constant observation and control. At the end of this process, the recruit and his or her style preferences have been transformed, ensuring that the new soldier will be able to contribute effectively to the nation's protection.

As a rule, corporations fail at similar transformational efforts because they do not have complete control of their employees' environments. In fact, they do not even have full control of the workplace environment. Work flows dictate whom people will see, what they will do, and with whom they will be friends. Any corporation that tried to control all of these factors would be out of business before any style transition had a chance to take effect.

Moreover, trying to force transitions in people's strategic styles has serious moral implications for organizations. Were such an effort successful, it could alter the entire structure of people's lives. A happily married employee, for example, might begin to experience style-incompatibility problems with his or her spouse, and the marriage be put in jeopardy. The very idea of organizations forcing transitions is thus a dangerous one. OE emphasizes an ethical viewpoint on change and improvement, and supports the contention that any employer now attempting to force style transition should quickly abandon such efforts.

THE PATH TO IMPROVEMENT

If organizations do not realize improvement through style transition, how *do* they realize it?

The answer was touched upon in Chapter 2. We cannot say that any strategic style is *intrinsically* good or bad, but we can say that every style has a distinctive contribution to make to an organization's long-term success. In this sense, all styles and all possible strategic profiles are good. Normally, once people know that, the door to improvement opens.

Experience with a thousand teams in real-life work situations has repeatedly demonstrated the power of this simple knowledge. People begin to see the value of other perspectives and are able to position themselves to support (or at least not to frustrate) a particular approach called for by a particular situation.

Merely explaining the strategic profile concept and showing people their own preferences is often enough

Figure 21. Speed of Organizational Death

One way of assessing the importance of each and every strategic style is to imagine what would happen if an organization lacked a particular style. The four styles are presented below in order of the speed of organizational decline and death.

Logical Processor

Fast demise. Examples of problems: mail will not be delivered, products will have uneven quality, paychecks are likely to be fraught with errors.

Reactive Stimulator

Medium-term demise. Over any reasonable length of time, the organization will face a vitally important situation that needs addressing without delay. Speed will be more important than exact methods. Without the RS, a timely response will likely be unavailable.

Hypothetical Analyzer

Medium- to long-term demise. Any organization will eventually need to make decisions involving serious commitments. Without the HA, it is likely that at least some of these decisions will be ill informed. Sooner or later, one of these missteps will cause organizational demise.

Relational Innovator

Long-term demise. The organization will find itself making buggy whips in the jet age. Alternatively, competitors will continually "eat its lunch" and the organization will starve to death.

to get immediate, visible improvements. From that point on, improvements can be made by "putting square pegs in square holes," effectively fulfilling the needs of a situation in order to realize material gains. The balance of this book will provide many more ways in which such gains can be realized to the benefit of all involved.

Figure 21 is a useful reference when explaining to employees and colleagues the respective strengths of the styles and their importance to long-term success. When organizations themselves do not recognize each style's contributory nature, they unwittingly speed their own decline—how quickly is illustrated in Figure 21.

LABELING ISSUES

Labeling is an issue that arises with any instrument that categorizes people. The basic concern is that a category will "stick" to a person, permanently labeling him or her. When this happens, the label takes precedence over a person's behavior, which is then always interpreted in whatever way necessary to conform to that label; what should be a basis for understanding becomes an inescapable trap of prejudgment. Categories which invite attributive valuation—that is, the polarities of negative–positive connotations—tend to encourage labeling. Obviously, this is a matter of high concern to people trying to improve organizational functioning.

However, not all categorizations lend themselves to permanent labeling, and not all invite attribution. OE ensures its categories fall into this group by doing the following:

1. Scaling the strategic styles so that all start from a central zero point. This creates a distinction in scales that discourages negative–positive connotations; it helps people see the styles as *different* from one another, rather than as relatively better or worse (see Chapter 2).

2. Naming the strategic styles in such a way that none sound particularly appealing and all prompt designation by initials. Both these characteristics are "neutralizing," and so encourage *neutral* valuation (see Chapter 2).

3. Stressing that all styles are good and all vital to success, whether long-term organizational success or group success at efforts of any complexity. People come to realize that tagging a style as "bad" reflects negatively *upon them,* as all styles are needed for success.

4. Clearly depicting all strategic styles in the Standard Graphic. As most people show some placement on each scale in the graphic, this discourages negative connotations — what a person might consider "bad" in someone else appears as a factor in his or her own profile!

5. Depicting the profile by linking the scales and creating quadrants. In this way, we do not isolate a person's placement on each scale, a form of profiling

which would suggest a more permanent condition of behavior—preferences that are "written in stone." As it is, the quadrants and their combined shape lend an *organic* dimension to the profile, rightfully suggesting that a person's style preferences *can* change—and we know they sometimes do, usually because of environmental factors. Permanent labels—the type we are concerned with—are less apt to develop.

Whether these tactics have proven highly effective, or whether OE by its very nature does not encourage labeling, extensive research has shown that permanent labeling simply does not happen in OE. In a recorded database of about 10,000 entries, there is not a single reported instance of labeling arising as an operational issue. Nor was an instance reported in more than 5,000 additional applications reviewed before that database began. These results were gathered from operating organizations in all geographic sectors, at all levels (from CEO to factory floor), and in all types of fields. Included were Fortune 500 firms, nonprofit associations, universities, and entrepreneurial startups. We can safely conclude, then, that labeling should pose no problem in either the understanding of or practical application of OE categories.

In this chapter, we covered the basics of predicting individual behavior and explored important issues associated with the strategic styles. To use this information properly, though, we must apply it to the proper focus of organizational engineering: group behavior. We must integrate the individual into a larger entity, the group, and show how group behavior can be predicted.

Chapter 4

PREDICTING
GROUP BEHAVIOR

THE INDIVIDUAL IS the elemental unit of an organization: without individuals, organizations cannot exist. However, we cannot explain, let alone improve, organizational functioning by focusing exclusively on these elemental constituents. Attempting to do so would be like trying to explain thought by focusing on the brain's individual neurons. Even perfect knowledge of a single neuron cannot explain an idea. An idea exists and has a life in the pattern of relations between neurons. The same holds true for teams, work groups, departments, divisions, and corporations. Organizations are founded on the working relationships between members, not the individual members in isolation. These relationships are as real as the individuals involved. To deny this is akin to saying that thinking is not real because it has no physical counterpart.

> **DEFINITION REVIEW**
>
> ➡ **PREDICTION**
> Show how group behavior can be reliably anticipated in advance

> **A SUBJECT MATTER OF ORGANIZATIONAL ENGINEERING IS THE RELATIONSHIPS BETWEEN STRATEGIC STYLE PROFILES.**

Thus far in this guidebook, we have investigated the information-processing model, have seen how it can be measured, and have applied the insights to individual behavioral prediction. Now it is time to learn how individual strategic profiles can be combined to produce accurate, reliable predictions of group behavior.

GROUP PREDICTION: THE BASIC PROCESS

Group behavior involves the interaction between and among individuals who, quite naturally, come to the group with information-processing strategies that have served them well in the past, and on which they continue to depend. From an OE point of view, we can say that the individuals' strategic profiles themselves interact, thus giving us a basis for prediction.

This process is most easily seen in the interactions of two people, the smallest group unit. As with any group, there are three fundamental stages:

1. Strategies Identification
2. Trial-and-Error Initiating
3. Mutual or Consensual Agreement

I. Strategies Identification

The first task confronting each person is to figure out where the other is "coming from" — to identify the other's strategies (see Figure 22). Strategic profiles are not "worn on the sleeve," and so must be discovered in the course

Figure 22. Strategic Profile Identification

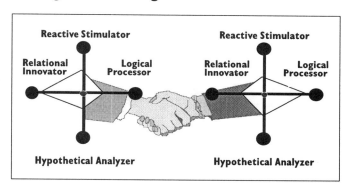

of interaction. The motive here is to avoid missteps later on by learning as much as possible about the other person's strategies now, during this initial period of social interaction.

Such motivation likely explains the common senior-level practice of introducing a new officer or director at a social event, rather than during the regular course of business. It gives people an opportunity to interact when the issues are trivial, the exposure is low, and the learning is high. Success during this interaction can help reduce style conflicts by setting the tone for and expectations of professional relations.

2. Trial-and-Error Initiating

While preliminary casual social interaction can help ease the transition to an effective working relationship, it is

Figure 23. Potential Resolutions: Distribution

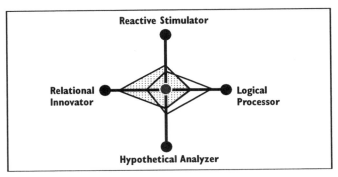

seldom enough to completely accomplish the job. This requires that the people involved actually engage in interactions which are focused on matters of common interest and in which, to a degree, they share a common destiny.

This stage of the interaction typically involves a trial-and-error initiative process. Each person begins offering various approaches to resolving the issue at hand. These approaches, as offered by one person, are represented in Figure 23 by the dot-filled profile on the left. Their distribution can be expected to follow the strategic profiles of the people involved. Assuming that a joint decision is required, this process can be expected to continue, usually with the initiative alternating between the people, until a mutually agreeable position on the issue is discovered.

3. Mutual or Consensual Agreement

This final stage represents the attainment of the pair's immediate purpose. In terms of strategic profiling, this agreement is likely to occur in the overlapping, *common area* of the members' profiles (see Figure 24). This area lies within the "comfort zone" of both individuals.

Of course, not every proposal falling within that zone will be automatically acceptable. Moreover, sometimes a proposal lying *outside* the zone will be acceptable if a compelling case can be made for its advantage. However, the mechanics of human information processing suggest that the selected proposal will fall within that zone, and indeed, most decisions fall into the common area of people's profiles. Understanding the power of this area is therefore vital to our predictions of group

Figure 24. Probable Zone of Agreement

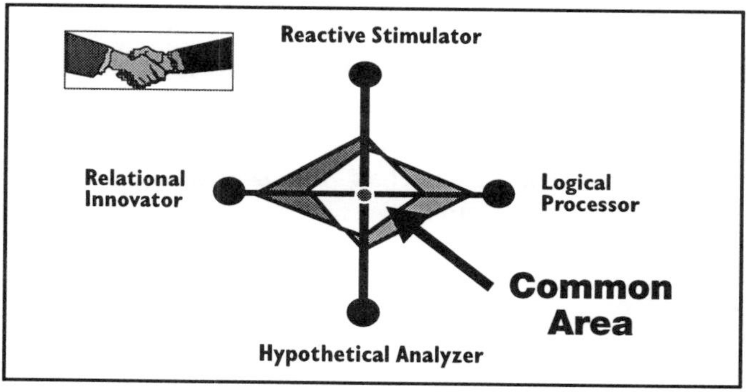

Reactive Stimulator

Relational Innovator

Logical Processor

Common Area

Hypothetical Analyzer

Figure 25. Strategic Style Contingency Table

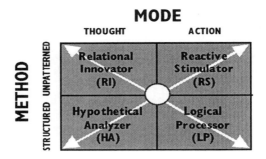

behavior. Let's take a closer look, continuing with our example of a two-person group.

THE COMMON AREA OF STRATEGIC PROFILES

Why People Seek the Common Area

To grasp why both members of our group would tend toward this area, we must consider what lies outside any common area: potentially mutually exclusive behavioral preferences. These contradictory preferences, if allowed expression, could compromise both individual and group effectiveness. They are perhaps best seen by collapsing the strategic profile into a standard contingency table, as shown in Figure 25.

The contingency table reminds us that each style is composed of different combinations of method and mode.

Styles that lie on the table's diagonal differ in *both* method and mode. Two people who occupy positions in opposing quadrants will thus see things very differently and be inclined to do things very differently. These differences translate into distinctive behavioral preferences, as shown in Figure 26.

Considering this situation, it is not difficult to see why the common area is sought. It is simply that area in which potential conflicts are minimized.

Large Common Areas

Profiles with large common areas suggest a "birds of a

Figure 26. Opposing Behavioral Preferences

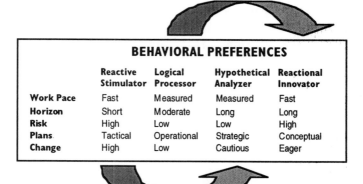

BEHAVIORAL PREFERENCES				
	Reactive Stimulator	Logical Processor	Hypothetical Analyzer	Reactional Innovator
Work Pace	Fast	Measured	Measured	Fast
Horizon	Short	Moderate	Long	Long
Risk	High	Low	Low	High
Plans	Tactical	Operational	Strategic	Conceptual
Change	High	Low	Cautious	Eager

Figure 27. Sample Large Common Area

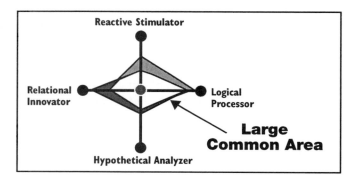

feather" type of relationship between people. The illustrative profiles in Figure 27 indicate that both individuals in our group tend to view the world using roughly the same horizon, are comfortable with about the same level of detail, are inclined to seek the same type of outcome, and so on. In essence, they are likely to see the same things, and miss the same things, in any given situation.

Whether a relationship with a large common area is, in practical terms, "good" or "bad" depends on the purpose of the group. If the group is seeking administrative efficiency and relatively rapid decision-making, it is "good." If the group is seeking the widest variety of options, it might be "bad." As we have seen earlier in this guidebook, there are no absolutes in such matters.

The existence of a large common area does not mean that synergy is low. There are many bases of synergy outside of information-processing styles. For example:

- *Education Level* — such as Ph.D., BS, high school
- *Educational Subject* — such as physics, chemistry, business, humanities
- *Biology* — such as gender, age, physical size
- *Upbringing* — such as cultural, socio-economic, geographic
- *Experience* — such as home life, work, hobbies

A sense of the actual distribution of large-common-area intersections might be obtained from actual field experience. The common area can be measured as the percentage of the strategic styles falling into that area. Using this measurement, the largest common area encountered has been under 80 percent for a two-person analysis. In larger groups with an average size of nine people, common areas in excess of 50 percent are seldom encountered.

Small Common Areas

A small common area may be seen as an example of an "opposites attract" condition (see Figure 28, which follows). Group profiles with such areas indicate that each member is addressing different aspects of the information-processing decision space; therefore, the range of options available to the group should be extensive. In

Figure 28. Sample Small Common Area

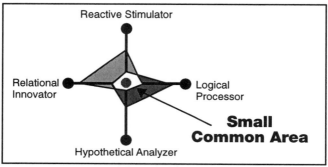

Reactive Stimulator

Relational Innovator

Logical Processor

Small Common Area

Hypothetical Analyzer

a range, managers might consider assigning to that group individuals whose combined profiles show a small common area.

However, such areas also indicate possible difficulties with maintaining internal relations. The small overlap means that each party will have to work harder to find a commonly acceptable means of addressing a decision issue. This can be expected to take its toll in tension and the time necessary to discover an acceptable position on the issue; thus administrative effectiveness will probably be low.

The probable net effect of low-level overlap is that the operational scope of the unit will be high, but at the price of low efficiency on the administrative end. Again, there is no inherent "good" or "bad" here. For some issues, the price is worth paying; for others, it is not. The role of the price is worth paying; for others, it is not. The role of the manager in OE is to identify the options and consequences, and then make rational tradeoffs.

The "Honest Broker" Strategy

Field experience has revealed many cases of the effective use of low-overlap relationships. These successful cases appear to rest on a foundation of mutual respect. With two-person units, this respect is usually founded on each party's understanding that the other is contributing a valuable quality or capacity unavailable within one's own behavioral repertoire. What seems to develop is a division-of-labor strategy whereby issues are allocated to the person most able to address them effectively.

While this strategy is efficient and effective, it lacks the full synergistic effect of two people working through an issue. The synergy occurs only at the front end of the process, where the initial allocation is made. There are methods, however, whereby more of the synergy can be preserved. One such method is the "honest broker" strategy, illustrated in Figure 29 (see next page).

This is a strategy borrowed from diplomacy. It involves introducing a neutral agent as a mediator or translator between two parties who might otherwise have difficulty communicating well and reaching agreement. In terms of information-processing facilitation, the important aspect of the honest broker is that he or she has "a foot in both camps." This allows the broker to understand the posi-

Figure 29. The "Honest Broker" Strategy

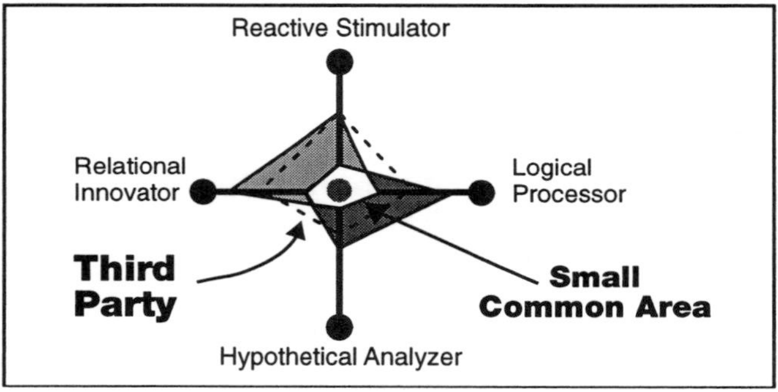

might be more acceptable to the other.

The "natural broker" role of people with balanced strategic styles is immediately apparent. Their profile indicates they automatically have a footing in all possible camps. This places them in a neutral position with regard to any strategic profiles that might be in play.

Of course, again there is a cost for every gain. In this case three people are doing the job of two. The value of the outcome might be worth the price, but there can be no universal assurance that this is the case.

Example of the "Honest Broker" Strategy in Action

The following situation occurred several years ago. An investment analyst and a product developer had to work together to prepare a large project for board-of-directors together to prepare a large project for board-of-directors approval. The analyst had a strong Perfecter pattern—a combination of idea-oriented RI and analytical HA. The developer had a strong Performer pattern—a pairing of action-oriented RS with procedurally inclined LP. Their relationship was tense and unpleasant. The developer sought out the analyst only when her input was absolutely necessary; the analyst tended to be adversarial because her attempted innovative contributions were summarily dismissed.

A higher-ranking manager assumed the broker role and invited the analyst and the developer to a meeting. The manager expressed appreciation for the skills of both individuals and cited specific examples of those skills, thus establishing his credentials as a neutral third party. Through a series of structured questions, the manager guided these parties into a conversation wherein each recognized and openly acknowledged the contributions of the other. Mutual respect was, to a degree, established.

Next, the analyst was asked to conduct a "live" analysis of a current project that the developer had underway. The analyst inputted variables into her computer model as the conversation proceeded (she was very adept at ad-lib analysis). The broker acted as translator, ensuring that the chance for misunderstanding was minimized, and continued to encourage each person to accept the other's contributions. This exercise was intended to help demonstrate the potential value of synergistic interaction.

It would be nice to report that the two people became fast friends. This did not happen. What did happen was that the intervention established an effective division-of-labor strategy between them. Though operational synergy was not realized, the hostility did cease. In this situation, the "honest broker" strategy served to teach individuals how to handle a small-common-area position. In terms of synergistic improvement, the value of the outcome was not worth the manager's continuing participation as a broker; in effect, a rational engineering tradeoff between cost and benefit indicated that the manager's time was more profitably spent elsewhere. Yet, the division-of-labor strategy had yielded a satisfactory improvement.

The Fractal Nature of Common Areas

A fractal is a geometric figure that can be subdivided (at least approximately) into a reduced-size copy of the larger whole from which it was drawn. Looked at another way, fractals can be combined to form larger figures that resemble the geometric structure of each constituent fractal.

Common areas have some fractal characteristics. Any geometric pattern that can be assumed by an individual's profile can be replicated by its common-area configuration with one or more other profiles. However, the profiles can overlap in such a way that the behavioral outcome *differs* from the preferences expressed by any constituent profile.

Figure 30. Divergent-Behavior Common Area

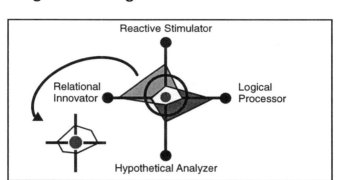

For example, in the two profiles shown in Figure 30, one member of the pair has a strong Changer pattern (upper left) and the other has a strong Conservator pattern (lower right). Yet the joint decisions made by the pair are likely to fall into the *Performer* quadrant (upper right), a shared strategic-pattern area. When making joint decisions, then, the two people will probably produce a behavioral pattern that is not readily apparent through an examination of their separate, individual profiles.

This type of outcome is common to almost everyone. Most of us have been involved with people with whom we have done things that neither we nor they would "ordinarily" do. This characteristic has important implications for the organizational engineer. It shows that it is possible to systematically obtain behavioral outcomes that do not appear to be inherent in the individual human assets available for the group undertaking.

Figure 31. Common Axis: No Common Area

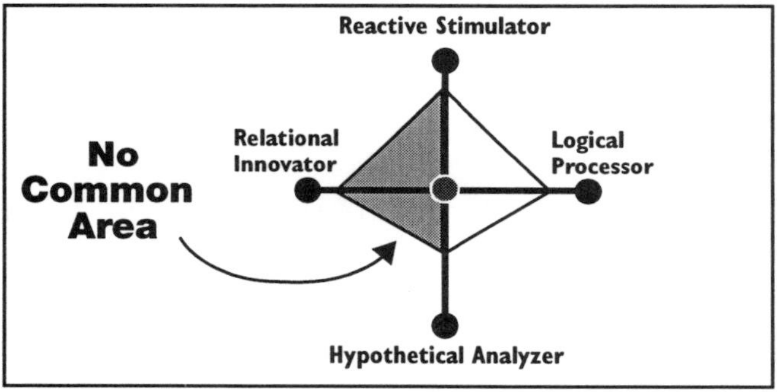

Common Axis

There are also situations where two or more people share a common axis but have no common area. This is illustrated in Figure 31. Here, both parties share a strong tendency to use a quick-reaction RS strategy. However, one is secondarily committed to the disciplined-action LP strategy, while the other is secondarily committed to the idea-oriented RI.

This condition is most likely an artifact of the "coarseness" of the measurement instrument that was used to create the individual profiles—the brevity of the instrument probably did not allow small degrees of other styles to register. The tradeoff for capturing these degrees would be to impose an extra administrative cost (in time and effort) on everyone who uses the instrument.

Regardless of whether the common axis is accurate or artifactual, the result is that both parties will tend to see merit in each other's principle strategic style. In some cases that single shared strategy will be sufficient to resolve the issue at hand. If it does not, the divergence in profiles will come into play. One person will be inclined to favor new, untested methods, while the other will prefer to rely on well-understood, proven solutions. Overall, the characteristics of such shared-axis profiles simply present a special case of the more typical low-common-area condition, and can be treated as such.

THE APPLICATION TO LARGER GROUPS

The principles that were here applied to two-person groups are equally applicable to larger groups. The common area would apply to groups governed by consensus decision-making. Decision strategies such as majority rule can be calculated by figuring out the areas in which at least 51 percent of the people involved occupy a position. The interpretation of the majority area is exactly the same as in the analysis of the two-person common area described in this chapter.

While the consensus area remains visible as people are added, alternative decision strategies become less clear (see Figure 32, which follows). A computer program is required to trace out the area of majority, super-majority, or other decision methods that might be used by a particular group. Use of a computer program reduces the tangle of intercepting profiles to a simple graphic resembling the

Figure 32. Example: Unanalyzed 12-Person Team

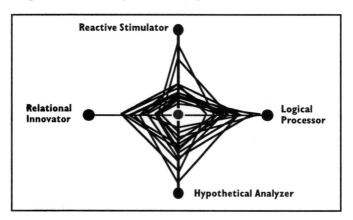

two-person composite profiles that we saw earlier in this chapter.

A sample profile of an analyzed 12-person group is presented in Figure 33. The white consensus area and outer perimeter of the profile are exactly the same as those in the two-person profiles reviewed earlier, only with more people included. The only real addition is the gray majority area.

The gray area is added because many groups use majority decision methods either explicitly or implicitly in their decision-making. For instance, in floating an initiative in a group, most people are sensitive to whether or not more members will be for it than against it. This alone

Figure 33. Example: Analyzed 12-Person Team

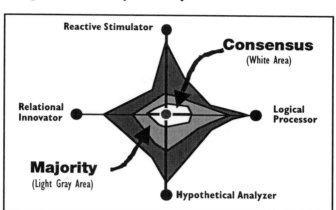

influences the frequency with which certain options will be offered and the intensity with which they will be pursued. And, of course, many groups explicitly adopt a majority-rule decision strategy to guide common efforts. Regardless of how it is used, the interpretation of the majority is exactly the same as that used for consensus.

NATURAL COALITIONS

Natural coalitions occur when two or more people view a situation in the same light and arrive at the same judgment of it. Coalitions can exert a disproportionate influence on a group, thus affecting prediction of group behavior. When people work together in this way, even inadvertently, they increase the brainpower available to refute or to support a position, are more attuned to capturing nuances, and so on. All of these assets are pointed at a relatively similar final outcome. The net result is that the influence of these natural groups is magnified beyond their absolute numbers.

One of the bases for a natural coalition is similarity in strategic profiles. This similarity suggests that the people involved are using similar decision horizons, are sensitive to the same level of detail, and seek approximately the same degree of certainty of outcome, among other things. This similarity of viewpoints increases the odds for the formation of a natural coalition.

In small groups potential coalitions are relatively easy to spot by the similarity of strategic profiles. In larger groups, however, an additional tool is needed—the centroid.

For purposes of organizational engineering, the centroid of a profile can be defined as the point best representing the entire profile—rather like the center of mass in physics from which the concept is borrowed. Operationally, it can be calculated as the center point of the four strategic styles that form the profile's boundary. It is similar to the average in ordinary arithmetic; its single point represents a larger distribution. The centroid will seldom correctly represent a particular event, but over a series of events, it will be more accurate than any other point. For identifying coalitions, the centroids of each individual profile can be calculated and posted to the composite profile of the

Figure 34. Illustration of a Potential Coalition

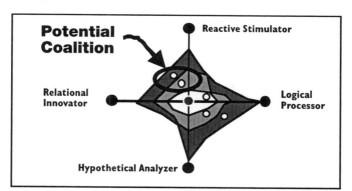

group. Figure 34 shows an actual five-person team with centroids included.

A close proximity of centroids alerts the organizational engineer to the potential for coalition formation. Viewed from this angle, the coalition is not considered a malicious or sinister manipulation of larger groups by subgroups; rather, it is regarded as a natural outcome of people seeing the same things and seeking the same kind of results. In effect, everybody can agree that the trees are blue because everybody is wearing blue glasses.

Like everything else in OE, coalitions are neither good nor bad in any absolute sense. If they further the group's objective, they can be seen as "good." If they frustrate it, they might be viewed as "bad." The centroid methodology can alert the manager and organizational engineer to the potential for coalition formation. An estimate of the value or exposure created can then be made in light of group objectives.

PREDICTIVE RULES OF THUMB

This chapter has shown how individual profiles can be combined to create group profiles. Group behavior can be predicted by applying the same basic principles that operate on an individual level. Some predictive rules of thumb for the strategic styles and patterns are provided below, and should prove highly useful to the manager interested in OE's effective application in the workplace.

PREDICTIVE RULES OF THUMB: STRATEGIC STYLES

- The dominant strategic style of an individual or a group is likely to be predictive of an initial response to an issue.

- The stronger a dominant style, the more likely the individual will persist in attempting to use it to resolve an issue at hand.

- The secondary strategic style of an individual or group is the next most likely response. It will probably be used if the issue does not yield to primary style solutions.

- The more a dominant strategic style exceeds the secondary style, the more likely the person's behavior will be fully characterized by that dominant style.

- The closer the dominant style is to the secondary style, the more likely it is that the person's behavior will be typified by the dominant strategic pattern.

- Split styles can be functional for the person holding them. They are not something to be corrected. Their effects, though, are something that the person with them should be made aware of.

- Strategic styles can change, but usually not rapidly. The older the measurement, the greater the potential for variance in predictive accuracy.

- Peripheral styles (those other than the primary or secondary styles) are usually significant only in group assessments, not in individual ones.

- Prediction should always be focused on a stream of decisions, not on any particular decision.

PREDICTIVE RULES OF THUMB: STRATEGIC PATTERNS

- Large common areas are generally favored in well-understood situations where operational effectiveness is heavily influenced by administrative efficiency.

- Small common areas are favored where issue options are incompletely defined and where provision has been made to accommodate group-integration issues.

- Strategic patterns are most useful in characterizing lengthy streams of decisions and overall strategic postures. Strategic styles are generally more useful in predicting transactional characteristics of individuals or shorter streams of decisions.

- Strategic patterns are measured by the surface area of a quadrant relative to the surface area covered in the other quadrants. The greater the divergence of the dominant pattern from the secondary pattern, the greater the expected predictive accuracy.

- Split patterns are identified by approximately equal surface areas lying on a diagonal from each other on the Standard Graphic. Split patterns are seldom functional in groups. They should alert the manager to the probability of tension in group dynamics.

- Close proximity of centroids only means there is a possibility of a natural coalition. However, the more divergent the cluster from the rest of the group, the greater the likelihood of actual formation.

The prediction of group and individual behavior is useful in its own right. However, the design parameters of OE require that we take still another step. We seek such prediction so we can guide groups toward the achievement of their objectives. Thus guidance options consistent with our information-processing perspective are the subject of the next chapter.

Chapter 5

GUIDANCE
PROVIDING SEMI-FIXED INITIATIVES

PREDICTION IS VALUABLE in its own right; however, for the purpose of organizational engineering, its real value is providing insight into the type of guidance that will help groups more fully achieve their objectives. OE focuses its guidance efforts on structural mechanisms that (1) affect performance

> **DEFINITION REVIEW**
>
> ➡ **GUIDANCE**
> Provide tools that allow group behavioral changes without requiring members to change their values, beliefs, or behavioral preferences

by regulating the relationships that exist, or could exist, within a group, and (2) lead to predictable, reproducible outcomes. Organizational engineers favor interventions that can be targeted at issues specific enough to offer a high probability of resolving (or at least ameliorating) the group vulnerability identified.

The scope of potential interventions is endless. For example, if a meeting is scheduled for 11 a.m., the patterns of behavior that people will start exhibiting at noon (lunchtime) are highly predictable. Also, if a large group is formed to address an issue, it is almost certain that individual contributions will be restricted by the time available to talk. Even seating arrangement affects interactive relations. Arrange seating in rows, and relationships appropriate to a lecture will be favored; arrange seating in a horseshoe, and more interactive relationships, appropriate to a seminar, will be favored.

The Principle of Structural Interventions

**Anything that patterns human behavior
in groups is a potential
structural-intervention tool**

INTERVENTION: TWO BASIC CATEGORIES

While the range of structural interventions is limited only by human imagination, it is useful to divide them into semi-fixed and flexible categories.

- **Semi-Fixed:** Interventions that, once installed, are difficult or expensive to change. Such interventions are the subject of this chapter.

- **Flexible:** Interventions that can be reversed relatively quickly with minimum cost. The subject of flexible interventions will be covered in Chapter 6.

Semi-fixed interventions are often, though not always, made by executive action rather than by group decision methods. The decision making is typically focused on, at most, a few individuals; thus, the organizational engineer and manager can have both greater influence and greater exposure in guiding choice.

SEMI-FIXED: GROUP FORM

Like people, organizations are information-processing entities. They too are subject to information overload, and must elect a structured or unpatterned approach in processing issue-relevant information. However, organizations can accomplish this by separating out component individuals to form a specialized unit to address the issue. The selection of these components will tend to favor different points on the continuum running from unpatterned to structured method. An example is illustrated in Figure 35.

In real life the distinctions suggested by this figure are not clear-cut, and hybrids are easily constructed. For instance, a large Midwestern telephone company uses

Figure 35. Organizational Form Versus Method

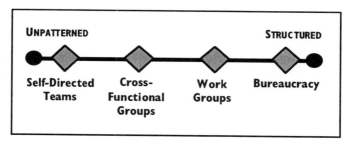

self-directed work teams for long-line construction. The teams are allowed to set schedules and hire contractors without consultation. However, when dealing with personnel, capital investment, and hiring matters, they are required to follow rigid procedures and hierarchical approvals. In effect, they are partially structured and partially unpatterned in form.

Generally, a team's form will be dictated by the nature of the environment in which the team will function. Unpatterned group forms are favored when issues are not well understood, pressures are uncertain, or the environment is volatile.

The unpatterned is well equipped for this because it brings no structural baggage. Essentially, everybody watches everything. Reaction time is fast, for there is no structure to impede action. Effectiveness is high because the team can take advantage of transient opportunities, has the capacity to accommodate unexpected pressures, and is able to redefine issues until success is realized. However, efficiency is usually lost because of redundancy (everyone watching everything), errors associated with fast reactions, and the loss of skills normally built through specialized focus. This is a simple tradeoff: efficiency is sacrificed for effectiveness.

Structured forms are favored under quite different conditions. If the environment is stable, if issues are well understood, and if pressures can be predicted accurately, then there is no need to sacrifice efficiency. Effective-

---

**EXAMPLE: AREAS OF POTENTIAL
ENVIRONMENTAL VOLATILITY**

- *Customers*
- *Suppliers*
- *Regulations*
- *Technology*
- *Legal Initiatives*

- *Competitors*
- *Internal Politics*
- *Employment Base*
- *Capital Availability*
- *Market Access*

---

ness can be obtained by the systematic execution of a known, well-understood method.

The basic OE strategy in guiding the selection of the group's organizational form is to examine the environment in which the group will work. The more uncertain the environment, the greater should be the inclination to recommend unpatterned forms.

DECISION METHODS

As in the case of group-form selection, the manager has a choice of group decision-making methods. Group decision-making techniques such as consensus, majority, and super-majority rule are the most common, with the hierarchical method perhaps the most used of the nongroup options. There is no universal preference here: each method carries with it particular costs and unique benefits.

The Hierarchical Method

The hierarchical method has the merit of being efficient, relatively consistent in outcome, and inexpensive. A sport such as football demonstrates that it can be used effectively in a team environment. The quarterback calls the play and the coach can fire players — strategies unmistakably hierarchical in character being applied in a venue that is clearly a team context.

Group effects are still in force even if the hierarchical option is elected. Experience proves, for example, that it is difficult for a leader to go against the universal opposition of his or her group. A method has been developed within OE to attempt to represent the degree of group-leader difference likely to be encountered. As illustrated in Figure 36, this method involves calculating the group's overall profile, the consensus area, and the majority area without considering the leader's strategic profile; then the leader's profile is superimposed on the group's. The difference between the leader's profile and that of the group's majority area (in dark gray) accurately describes the difficulty a leader will encounter in moving a group toward his or her preference.

Our figure indicates the leader is "pulling" the group in the same direction it is naturally inclined to go — the LP Strategic Option. The leader is likely to be seen as a bit more aggressive in pursuit of a commonly acceptable goal, but in all likelihood the leader will largely get his or her way. Thus, the same character of

Figure 36. Sample Leader–Group Effects

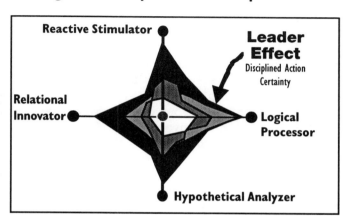

decision will be realized with lower cost and higher efficiency than if group processes were relied upon.

Of course, a leader's effect can be diametrically opposed to the group's inclinations. In that case, it is likely that neither the leader nor the group will be able to realize their expectations. Instead, all will experience frustration.

Consensus and Majority Rule

Of the group decision-making techniques, consensus and majority rule are the most commonly encountered. These are typically recognized as being more expensive in terms of time and psychological energy than hierarchical methods, but at least in some cases, they are thought to carry benefits of "commitment" that offset the cost.

While the value of commitment cannot be measured, the probable cost can be estimated. The smaller the total surface of the consensus or majority area relative to the total area of the group profile, the greater the expected difficulty in arriving at a group decision. Essentially, the smaller the area of group overlap, the larger and more certain are costs that will offset the effect of commitment.

Mechanically applying predesignated "best" ways can expose groups to unexpected vulnerabilities. Figure 37 shows the profile of a real team that was analyzed using OE methodology. The consensus area describes a split style for the group; this means the group is apt to vacillate between careful study and spontaneous action. Another group that uses the output of this group as their input could pay a serious price for the gain in "commitment."

Such a profile also provides information on the likely character of group decisions. For example, with the team profiled in Figure 37, the majority-rule method would likely result in decisions following the Performer pattern (an RS-LP combination). If this pattern serves the team's objectives, the majority-rule strategy could be worth considering. In addition, the majority area (in gray) is fairly large and the "cost" of reaching a major-

Figure 37. Sample Split-Style Group Profile

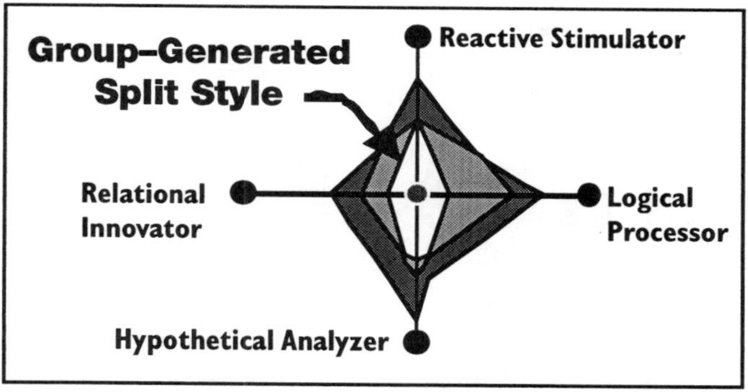

Group–Generated Split Style — (arrow)

● Reactive Stimulator

Relational Innovator ●

● Logical Processor

Hypothetical Analyzer ●

ity decision is likely to be low. Under these conditions, we might see the gain in commitment as almost a bonus.

In summary, when selecting the decision method, we should consider the expected cost of the decision process in both time and psychological energy. We should also consider the compatibility of the likely decision direction of the group relative to its objectives. All of this information is easily available from a visual review of the group's profile. There is no "magic bullet" here. Instead, we have a reliable, accessible engineering method that can guide our rational choice.

Figure 38. Size Distribution of Actual Teams

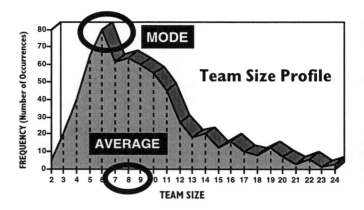

GROUP SIZE

Group size is a relatively uncomplicated variable. Generally, the larger the size, the more difficult it is to coordinate different actions among group members. Our OE database indicates that successful large groups are typically single-function entities doing relatively simple, repetitive tasks.

The largest single group in our database was composed of 60 people functioning under a single supervisor. The group worked in the packing section of a warehouse, and everyone had a roughly similar job. The supervisor sat in a glass office in the middle of the floor, which gave him easy access to all of the people reporting to him.

However, this was an unusual case. More commonly, once a group's size exceeds 12 to 15 people, the group has an almost automatic tendency to break up into functionally distinct subgroups.

Figure 38 shows the distribution of team sizes drawn from the database. The mode, or most frequently encountered group size, is about five people. The average is about nine people. Therefore, field experience suggests that most organizations have found that groups with five to nine people are the most effective.

Regarding group size, it is recommended that managers consider the complexity of the task in terms of the coordination demanded between team members. The more complex the task, the smaller the size of the operational group should be, thus easing coordination burdens.

ADJUSTING GROUP COMPOSITION

Adjustment—adding, deleting, or substituting group members—is perhaps the most frequently encountered semi-fixed initiative applied to existing groups. Almost everyone will agree that changing the composition can dramatically affect the performance of the group. The preparation of a group strategic profile will reveal how much of a change can be expected as well as the probable direction of the change.

Like the other semi-fixed initiatives, changing the composition of a group is a serious matter. A manager can do such things as:

- Reweigh the composite and thereby change the direction of group decisions
- Introduce new options into the group decision matrix
- Create or strengthen the operation of a coalition
- Bar consensus by adding people holding strongly to perspectives that refuse to admit options of a particular type

The adjustment strategy can produce relatively certain results and is particularly well suited to the engineering of established groups. However, it is a semi-fixed option, and thus should be approached with care. The result is likely to "live" with the group for a considerable time.

RULES OF THUMB: SEMI-FIXED INITIATIVES

- These initiates should be used with care. The results are durable. They should be worth the investment of time and resources in both selection and deployment.

- Examine the issue environment of the actual or anticipated group. If it is volatile, unstable, or poorly understood, then favor unpatterned group forms (e.g., teams, matrix, cross-functional). If it is stable and well understood, then favor structured alternatives (e.g., work groups, hierarchical systems).

- If the nature of the group's work requires frequent decisions, consider hierarchical decision methods because of their efficiency.

- If the group overlap (consensus or majority) is reasonable and the work will benefit significantly from personal commitment, then consider group methods. The lower the overlap, the higher the expected "commitment" benefit should be.

- When using group methods, consider matching the direction of the overlap to the type of group decisions being used. Favor decision methods that bias the group toward strategies that support goal achievement.

- When determining group size, evaluate the similarity of the tasks performed within the group. The more dissimilar the tasks necessary to achieve the group's goals, the smaller the group size should be, thus minimizing the coordination burden.

- When adding, deleting, or substituting group members, consider the effect of this action on the strategic bias and decision structure. Changes should further (or at least not frustrate) the mission of the group.

Chapter 6

GUIDANCE
PROVIDING FLEXIBLE INITIATIVES

WE HAVE SEEN THAT GUIDANCE can be provided to groups in the form of semi-fixed initiatives. Like those interventions, flexible initiatives are targeted at creating predictable, reliable patterns of human behavior in group settings. The difference between them is one of degree rather than kind. The

> **DEFINITION REVIEW**
>
> ➡ **GUIDANCE**
> Provide tools that allow group behavioral changes without requiring members to change their values, beliefs, or behavioral preferences

most notable feature of flexible interventions is that they can be changed or reversed relatively quickly and without incurring a high cost.

Flexible initiatives can be introduced through a wide variety of mediums, informal as well as formal. For example, group norms are a form of structural adjustment. Norms tend to evolve through the generalization of behavior patterns displayed in the group context. No one really chooses norms—they just naturally "appear." Once in place, they pattern behavior as certainly as do directly selected mechanisms.

While informal mechanisms play a part in group functioning, organizational engineering primarily focuses on interventions that can be consciously chosen and whose implementation produces results that are predictable. The list of flexible interventions is virtually endless. However, certain types do reoccur, and so warrant discussion in this chapter. We can categorize these as:

- **Rules**
- **Roles**
- **Process**
- **Knowledge**
- **Task Structure**
- **Goals and Objectives**
- **Allocation Strategies**
- **Subteams**

Other guidance mechanisms such as facilities and sponsorship will also be discussed.

RULES

Rules are preprogrammed responses to situations. They are simple to declare and are usually easily understood by those involved. In operational settings, rules tend to be the first response to changing group behavior. Used with discretion, they are a powerful tool; used inappropriately they can lead to dysfunctional outcomes.

As the characteristics shown in Figure 39 suggest, rules are most favored in well-understood, stable situations. In these cases, the value of response options is known and rules can be targeted to realize the most advantageous of those options. Stability means that rule inflexibility may be only a small detriment.

Figure 39. General Characteristics of Rules

➡ **Quick to install.** Usually declaration and approval is all that is required.

➡ **Action-oriented.** Viewable action is required to monitor compliance.

➡ **Highly efficient.** Rules tend to be stable and can be optimized through incremental adjustment.

➡ **Certain in outcome.** Rules tend to define consequences as part of their structure.

➡ **Inflexible.** Rules tend to be dogmatic in character and usually do not handle "gray" areas well.

➡ **Mechanical in application.** The use of rules tends to discourage the full consideration of all aspects of a situation.

For an example of the effective application of a rule-based solution, we can turn to the experience of a government aerospace contractor. The firm "low-balled" a government-contract bid, which was subsequently accepted. A team of engineers was then formed to figure out how the product could be built with the dollars available.

The team had an overall HA-LP orientation. They were highly skilled at analysis and cautious in approach. RI capabilities were concentrated in a few members; thus, new and even radical ideas were available. However, when these ideas surfaced, the strong analytical capabilities of the HA immediately detected potential "exposures." The strong LP component tended to resist the more innovatively aggressive elements, since they could not be readily tied to existing practices. The net effect was that ideas were killed as fast as they were put on the table.

An organizational analysis revealed the vulnerability of the group posture, and members agreed on the following:

RULE TO ENCOURAGE NEW IDEAS

This team has the analytical power to quickly identify exposures, and this could result in prematurely discounting otherwise viable ideas. The team will therefore adopt a rule that extends the time period over which an idea is considered. New ideas will be treated seriously and will "live" for at least two team meetings. At the first meeting every team member must make at least one positive statement or recommendation (no negatives allowed). At the second meeting, the idea can be killed.

This rule changed the orientation of the team members. Analytical talent was turned toward making the required positive contribution. The cautionary tendencies were tempered by the same need.

The rule met the conditions of an effective strategy. The situation was well understood, with minimal intervening variables. Inflexibility was not a detriment, for the situation was stable and the rule was designed to fit it. The net result? The rule worked and the team met its objective.

When considering rules, the manager should keep in mind that many rules can be fashioned to address the same condition. In the example below, two somewhat different rules have been structured toward the same end-result. Here, the rules are worded as the manager would propose them to the team; members would then make the decision of which proposal to adopt (if either is acceptable to them), and what specific rule to set.

EXAMPLE OF ALTERNATIVE RULES
TO ENCOURAGE RISK TAKING

Possible Rule:
The conservative nature of the LP-HA can create a bias against risk taking. If the team finds this is the case, it may want to adopt a rule that requires accepting more risk than the team is naturally inclined toward. For instance, this rule might state that no analytical or time resources will be spent on issues that have a trivial downside risk. The probable greater failure rate of issues resolved under this rule would be considered the price of the savings in team resources (analytical resources as well as the team's time commitments).

Possible Rule:
This team will probably be inclined toward adopting low-risk strategies. Such strategies will be inappropriate for many, if not most, of the issues the team confronts. Thus, members might benefit from adopting a strategy that "forces" the team to accept a higher than "natural" risk when dealing with certain situations. For instance, the team might choose to defer to the riskier option on close votes or controversial issues. In short, the team might consider developing a slight bias in favor of more risk.

Providing alternative suggestions increases the odds of acceptance because nuances of difference can matter. The usual result in actual field operations is that the group grasps the basic idea and creates their own rule, one more directly targeted at its objectives and more fully accommodating of its unique circumstance. This approach serves to increase the compliance commitment to the newly adopted rule.

Rules are usually favored as a governance device by people who employ a structured information-processing strategy (the analytical HA and the process-inclined LP). Once accepted, compliance is usually not an issue. The same cannot be said for people with unpatterned strategies (the action-oriented RS and the idea-generating RI). To them, rules are just one more unpatterned factor that may or may not be seen as relevant. Field experience suggests such individuals will accept rules but probably not follow them with any degree of consistency.

Generally, rules represent a structured approach to group alignment. They are best used in cases where . . .

— structured strategies dominate the group

— the issue is well understood and the effect of the response options can be accurately assessed

— the probability of encountering "gray" areas of applicability is low

— the condition being addressed is likely to persist over time

— the chances of unexpected variables intervening to
   affect the issue are low

ROLES

Roles are assignments of accountability for and authority
regarding an end or a condition. Roles specify a result
without prescribing exactly how the result is to be realized. In OE, roles focus on the governing of the relationships that are imbedded in the group's construction.
Some general characteristics of roles are shown in
Figure 40.

Figure 40. General Characteristics of Roles

➡ **Low efficiency.** They are rethought for every
   application.

➡ **Greater situational sensitivity.** Their content
   can be "tailored."

➡ **Outcome is less certain.** This is because of their
   content variability.

➡ **More personal.** There is greater accommodation
   of personal preferences in execution.

➡ **End result-focused.** This contrasts with the
   process focus of rules.

Roles have many purposes. One significant purpose is to offer the individual group member a "shield" against criticisms that might otherwise be directed at his or her position on an issue. The unpopularity of a position can arise simply because of other members' strategic predispositions. If left unprotected, the individual might be unwilling to offer the group a particular perspective or to express a negative option.

A particularly noteworthy instance of this phenomenon occurred at a major bank in the Southwest. A team had been convened to outline a reengineering plan for the bank's backroom operation. An organizational analysis revealed that all team members but one were strong idea-generating RIs. That single exception was a strong analytical HA.

The overwhelming dominance of the RI component created a meeting character whereby ideas quickly rebounded between members, often heading down paths not central to the team's mission. Certain ideas captured the interest of members and were quickly solidified into recommendations, usually without critical examination. Through all this, the lone HA sat in silence.

Organizational analysis revealed the team's tendency to lose focus and its bias toward uncritically accepting interesting ideas. Members agreed to establish the role of "Criticizer" to offset this tendency, and awarded it to the lone analytical HA. The role required that the HA offer any and all objections, concerns, reservations, and uncertainties she could think of, prior to group acceptance of an item.

The Criticizer role was given both charter and mandate. It was intended to stop the ever-accelerating whirlwind of ideas long enough to introduce an element of critical, disciplined thought into the process; but it also shielded the HA from being termed a "wet blanket." Now her duty to the group was to offer evaluation, assessment, and judgment from her unique perspective. It is worth adding that the team went on to make an outstanding contribution, one noted by the bank's entire senior management staff, up to and including the board of directors.

Comparing roles and rules

Roles are more personal than rules, and their execution can be "bent" to more fully accommodate the situations in which they are applied. Because they do not prescribe exactly what is to be done, they tend to be more acceptable to people with unpatterned strategies (the action-oriented RS and idea-founded RI). Instead of seeing the role as just another unpatterned factor passing by (the RS and RI view of rules), these people tend to view it as an objective to be served by the collection and assembly of unpatterned factors. They are allowed the discretion to apply their favored strategy within the overall framework of satisfying role responsibilities.

The choice between roles and rules as a means of governing relationships can be seen as a tradeoff. Almost anything that can be accomplished by a rule also can be addressed by a role. Like rules, roles have the merit of being fast to install, reliable in performance, and easy to discard if they prove unneeded. Also like rules, they must be taken seriously by everyone to work effectively.

Roles are usually preferable to rules in cases where . . .

— the unpatterned strategic styles (RS and RI) are favored by the group

— the situation being addressed is unstable or poorly understood

— efficiency in execution is not an important component of group success

— a variation in the certainty of outcome can be tolerated

Constructing Roles

The general formula for constructing roles involves five steps:

1. Identify a vulnerability of the group as a whole (not necessarily individual members).

2. Structure a "job" whose fulfillment will offset the identified vulnerability.

3. Obtain agreement that the role is needed and that its execution will serve the best interests of the group.

4. Name the role so members can refer to it during group discussion.

5. Publicly award the role to one or more group members on either a permanent or a rotating basis.

In the course of developing the OE discipline, many roles have been constructed to meet the unique situations encountered among the groups analyzed. Examples of those roles are provided below.

EXAMPLES OF OE-CONSTRUCTED ROLES

"Specifier" Role

The group may have a tendency to leave "loose ends" when it comes to specifying the step-by-step instructions needed to put a proposal into actual practice. If this is seen as a vulnerability, the group may want to consider using the "Specifier" role.

The person occupying this role would be required to identify areas where a proposal may require operational specification (step-by-step instruction) before implementation. The purpose of the Specifier role is to ensure the group considers the "ground level" details of the proposals in question. The group may override the Specifier, but it must hear this person before a proposal is accepted.

"Assessor" Role

If a team tends to overinvest in analysis, and its members judge this to be an exposure, the "Assessor" role may help solve the problem. This role's purpose is to interrogate analytical assignments and ensure they are appropriate for the issue at hand.

For example, the person in this role may be required to question the status of all outstanding analytical assignments at each meeting. The focus might include an update on cost, expected return, and desirability of continuing the study. This process is intended to keep the team alert to the cost and expected returns on an analysis on a marginal basis (i.e., the value of remaining work relative to the expected value of that work).

"Venturer" Role

The group may be vulnerable to "automatically" opting for relatively risk-free options. If the group attributes this vulnerability to a fear of exposure, it might want to consider adopting the role of "Venturer."

The person in this role might be charged with proposing and defending the more aggressive options available. To ensure that the options are considered, the group could be required to explicitly reference the Venturer before a final decision is concluded.

"Braking" Role

This team may have a tendency to move too rapidly toward implementation. If the group considers this to be a concern, it may want to use the "Braking" role.

The role incumbent would be required to offer reasons for the delay of any rapid implementation initiatives offered within the group. Elaboration could be added. For example, the Braking person could be authorized to poll team members and ask questions such as "What is the best reason you can offer for this delay?" A process like this might help the group get a better perspective on the value of immediate action.

"Discussion Director" Role

The group may find that it would benefit from the role of "Discussion Director."

The person charged with this role might be required to intervene if he or she deems the discussion to be diverging from the subject. Upon intervention, group members could be polled to determine if they concur with the judgment. Using this strategy, the Discussion Director acts as a signaling mechanism rather than as a manager. Usually, strong RIs can be returned to the subject merely by breaking the compounding spirals of ideas catalyzing other ideas.

PROCESS

Process interventions involve installing one or more activities whose execution will offset a known vulnerability. For instance, the activity of following an agenda helps ensure that items of importance to the group will be addressed. Similarly, the practice of scheduling meetings to occur on the first Monday of every month lends continuity to the life of a group.

OE process interventions come in various forms. In one of the most frequently used interventions, group members are given a series of structured questions that they must answer before committing to an issue-related activity or goal. The sample questions presented in Figure 41, which follows, are intended to offset the tendency of a strongly analytical HA group to invest in more analysis of an issue than is warranted by the issue's value. Similar questions can be designed to offset any other identified structural vulnerability of a group.

In field situations groups seldom accept all of the questions offered; instead, they pick and choose among them. They also use the questions as a catalyst for designing other questions that more closely fit their particular circumstances. A key to facilitating this process is to start off the group with enough questions to ensure that most members will find something to which they can relate and which they can accept. Such activity usually initiates a dialogue that culminates in the group accepting some subset of the questions offered.

Figure 41. Process Questions to Offset Overinvestment in Analysis

- *What is the probability that we will miss something important if we apply a lesser standard to this activity?* (That is, is the pickup in knowledge likely to have a payoff in excess of its cost?)

- *How much could it "cost" the organization if we were to apply a lesser standard of rigor and miss something in this area?* (This asks for an estimate of the maximum exposure without assigning a probability to its occurrence.)

- *If we charge for achieving the proposed goal, will anyone pay for it?* (The "payment" should include a provision for the equivalent of "profit." If all that is being returned is the endeavor's cost, the activity could be considered "break-even." Few organizations can continue to exist on a break-even strategy.)

- *Is there a product in the market that could reasonably satisfy the need? Is it worth our time "inventing" a replacement?* (The team will likely be good at identifying deficiencies in existing products. It may not be so good at evaluating the worth of the "pickup" from tailoring them to the organization's unique needs. This question helps to focus the team on the materiality of such deficiencies.)

- *If the time available to us were cut by 10 percent, would we be able to relax our standards in this area?* (If the answer is yes, the team may want to consider whether the savings should be made without the need for external stimulus.)

- *If I owned the firm, how much would I pay to know the details we are proposing to collect?* (The activity might be questioned if everyone on the team cannot answer this positively.)

- *Is this activity material [or critical] enough to our mission for us to pursue the detail we're proposing?* (If not truly material, the team may want to consider whether this is an "overkill" situation.)

- *Which of our goals does this proposed activity address? Is it a high-priority goal?* (This type of question helps the team avoid devoting too many resources to secondary objectives.)

- *What is the minumum amount of analysis and assessment we could "get away with"?* (If a figure in dollars or hours is attached to this, the figure could operate as a baseline. Increases over this line could then be justified by their incremental contribution.)

- *Did we hear the minority view?* (The team has strong disciplined assets. Such postures may exclude viable options that do not conform to the group's standards. This question helps ensure that the group actually "heard" those options and that the decision to exclude them is based on sound logic, not just strategic preference.)

- *Is this goal worth the effort we are planning to expend on it?* (This team tends to overplan and overspecify. What starts out as a reasonable proposal may get so enhanced that the expected return could never offset the cost. Calling attention to this possibility helps the team avoid "creeping commitment inflation.")

- *Can we take a "baby step"?* (The team may be inclined to see things in all of their complexity and to try to resolve all issues in one stroke. This question alerts the team to partial options that may solve "enough" of the issue.)

Field experience suggests that structured questions are among the most generally useful of the process strategies. Experience also suggests that structured questions are most accepted in groups containing appreciable elements of multiple strategic styles. Each style involved seems drawn to certain questions, perceiving some gain in them, and tends to sponsor them, perhaps with some modification. Even when the activity suggested by the questions is not adopted, the questions appear to influence the group in positive ways.

Other process-type interventions can be devised to meet the group's specific needs. For example, a group heavily biased toward instant action might install a review process that would automatically slow response time. A group heavily inclined toward analysis might install a "bidding" activity whereby leadership on an issue is awarded to the person who "bids" the shortest delivery time. A central point is that we can offset or at least temper some group vulnerabilities by constructing activities designed to offset the exposure identified.

Overall, process interventions are subtler in operation than are roles and rules. Over time, they tend to evolve into group norms and the reason why they were installed tends to fade. Being subtle, they are usually less powerful in directing group behavior than are roles and rules. Yet they have their place in our toolbox.

KNOWLEDGE

Most people have difficulty seeing beyond the standards implied by their own strategic styles: they tend to believe that everyone should think and act as they do. Consequently, variations from those standards are typically seen as errors, deficiencies, or incapacity. Eventually, attributions come into play. Individuals with other styles may be regarded as "pig-headed," "scatterbrained," "terminally slow," "analytically paralyzed"; these or any of myriad similar attributions may be used to "explain" the discrepancies between personal standards.

Knowledge of information-processing styles is generally the most powerful tool for redirecting this negative energy into a positive force. The application of the tool requires only that everyone in the group be given the results of his or her information-processing assessment. When people understand that the different behaviors they see in others are simply a necessary consequence of legitimate information-processing strategies, their inclination to make negative attributions is defused. Good-natured discussions between group members follow almost automatically. Reason replaces ridicule and insight dissolves intolerance.

A most telling instance of the use of the knowledge method was reported by a consultant working with a large group at a health insurance provider in South Carolina. Animosities within the group had grown into almost open hostility. At first, the group leader (a strong RS-RI) was the focal point of much of the antagonism, but now everyone was angry with everyone else. The situation was a mess.

The consultant administered the information-processing assessment to all group members. He then met with the leader to explain the results and plan the next step. The leader reacted almost instantly and called a meeting for the next morning to be attended by all of her staff—the RS style is not known for patience.

When people arrived the next morning, they found the chairs in the meeting room had been arranged in a circle and the tables had been removed. A single chair was set in the center of the room. As they entered, they were given a printout of their own report. The eight-page report contained the information outlined below.

CONTENT OF INDIVIDUAL ASSESSMENT REPORT

- **Primary Style Identification:**
  Common Characteristics (*priorities, decision horizon, approach*)
  - ❖ Typical needs (*conditions for optimal functioning*)
  - ❖ Goal preferences/considerations
  - ❖ Directional guidance preferences
  - ❖ Supervision preferences
  - ❖ Appreciation (*e.g., social-reward preferences*)
  - ❖ Organization (*personal preferences*)
  - ❖ Detail orientation
  - ❖ Acceptance/Sponsoring of change

- **Secondary Style Identification**
- **Strategic Style Profile**
- **Best Learning Strategies for the Individual Style**
- **Working with People Using Other Strategic Styles**
- **Best Indicated Organizational Environment**
- **Strengths Associated with the Individual Style**
- **Contributions of Others to Performance**
- **Listening to People Who Use Other Strategic Styles**
- **Talking to People Who Use Other Strategic Styles**

The leader entered the room last and took the seat in the center of the circle. Using her individual report as a script, she proceeded to recite her information needs, communication preferences, goals, capabilities, and so on. The consultant sat in the corner of the room with his mouth open. When finished, the leader simply sat down.

Without any prompting or facilitation, the others stood up and, following her example, recited their own preferred methods and style-related needs. After everyone had been given a chance to speak, the leader stood up, thanked everyone, and closed the meeting. She provided no guidance on what to do next, no summarization of lessons learned, no anything. That was it.

The next morning the consultant circulated among the staff members who had attended the meeting. The response was awesomely positive. People who had been antagonistic were found talking to each other. One person who spoke with the consultant described the change as a "miracle." Of course, the consultant was pleased and did not hesitate to take credit for planning the experience.

It should be cautioned that although the above is a useful example, it does *not* reflect the optimum approach to such a situation. The recommended approach involves the following steps:

1. Pass out the completed individual reports, and allow time for people to read them.

2. Provide a "thumbnail" explanation of the theory.

Explain that the report is merely an expression of information-processing preferences and that it says nothing about personality or other private matters.

3. Ask people if they agree with their reports. Face validity is extremely high and agreement is the norm. If there are disagreements, they usually center on minor matters and can be dismissed with the question "Do you substantially agree?"
   In the rare event that people do not, simply ask them to explain how they prefer to get information and what things they need to process it. (Essentially, refer to the subheadings in the report).

4. Facilitate a discussion on what the results mean for group functioning. The increased level of understanding usually translates into a willingness to accommodate the needs and preferences of the others in the group.

The results of the process appear durable. For example, in a follow-up study of a session similar to the one above, the Director of Organization Development for a major Midwestern industrial firm found that 18 months after the session, people were still using the insights and the nomenclature of HA, RI, LP, and RS in their daily activities—even at the lunch table.

In summary, the awareness that there are different, equally legitimate strategic styles, and that the styles are founded on nothing more than methods of information processing, is usually sufficient to produce an immediate gain for all involved. The power of this simple strategy should not be underestimated. It often turns out to be the single most powerful guidance strategy.

TASK STRUCTURE

This is an infrequently used but helpful technique. It involves breaking the task of the group down in a way that offsets an inherent group vulnerability. For instance, during the development of this methodology, we had occasion to work with a major provider of computer software services. The firm was engaged in a reengineering effort at a 2000-employee site. Their strategy was to "borrow" people from all over the nation, fly them in for a six-week stint, and then release them back to their home location.

The assessment of one team indicated a composition of eight extreme instant-action RS styles. The team had been assigned to an "as is" effort that involved the careful documentation of what was in place before reengineering was applied. We knew such a detail-sensitive, methodical activity was not an ideal match for the spontaneous, unpatterned, detail-adverse preferences of the RS; so we blew the whistle.

Because it was too late to substitute people, a system was devised whereby task focus was rotated through the team: each member would work for one week on a particular activity, then turn it over to one teammate and receive a "new" activity from another. There was a degree of redundancy here, as each time someone took over a partially completed activity, he or she had to review the other person's work to "come up to speed." However, although the process was somewhat inefficient, the work was done correctly and the team's mission was accomplished.

Another case worth noting involved an engineering team of strongly analytical HAs who worked for an automobile manufacturer. The team was charged with generating engineering solutions for difficult tradeoffs required to move a certain style of car from design status to manufacturing status. Whenever they presented their work to management, every comment would give rise to additional analytical work that "should" be considered. By the time a presentation reached its conclusion phase, the conclusion had "disappeared." Everybody was frustrated over the lack of progress.

The OE consultant for the group suggested one small change. The task of presentation was redesigned. The engineers presented their conclusions first, and then provided the supporting reasons for those conclusions. Comments made during their presentations now became challenges to analytic quality—usually a matter of high value to someone who takes pride in clarity of reasoning and quality of judgment. Rather than subjects to be studied, the comments were now questions to be answered—and on the whole they were answered, in a time frame acceptable to other teams charged with acting on the engineering team's results. Everyone was a lot happier.

Task-structure-related guidance and interventions are almost always specific to a particular group and the task assigned to the group. There are really no general rules of thumb in this area. However, awareness that the task itself is a potential organizational-engineering variable may alert practitioners to use such guidance if the opportunity presents itself.

GOALS AND OBJECTIVES

Goals and objectives are the fundamental "glue" of the group effort. They provide people with a reason for working together, and can determine the required character of group coordination. They distinguish a team from a crowd.

The Importance of Magnitude

Academic research and practical experience identify the nature of a group's goals as the single most important component leading to success. Challenging goals naturally bind the group into a single entity, for they require the contribution of all involved. If some group members lack such a commitment, it is likely that other members will make a concerted effort to "bring them back in line." The "glue" is strong because challenging goals motivate members to keep it strong. The greater the number of motivated members, the stronger the "glue."

The Scope of Goals and Objectives

Scope is another aspect of goals that is worth considering,

for it often lends focus and direction to a group activity. Narrow goals tend to focus activity narrowly. For example, a goal of "servicing clients within one day of a call" focuses the group on a short-term time frame and tangible outcomes. The specific character typical of narrow goals tends to make them favored by those whose profiles fall toward the "action" end of the method/mode continuums—the RS and LP strategic styles.

Broad goals diffuse the focus. For instance, if the goal is "to become best in class," the group will probably consider many variables as it searches for what constitutes the "best," who is the competition, and how the magnitude of the gap might be measured. The ambiguous and imprecise nature of the goal is well suited to the thought-based strategies of the RI and HA styles.

The Importance of Environment

Depending upon the group's predominant strategic style, members will favor either narrow goals or broad ones. Neither is right or wrong. Both can be challenging. However, the key to the most appropriate type of goal is not the group's strategic preference; rather, it is the nature of the environment in which the group operates.

If the environment is stable, then important determinants of group success can usually be isolated, identified, and depended upon. Here narrow, well-targeted goals would likely be preferred. Their tight focus can help the group reach a level of excellence unobtainable if the group's energy were diffused.

Conversely, if the environment is unstable, broader goals and objectives are in order. Rapidly changing conditions can negate the value of tight, highly defined goals, sometimes without the change even being noticed. Broad goals allow the group to pick up changes at an earlier point and act to take advantage of them.

The following case illustrates the importance of environment in setting goals. A firm that heat-treats metal launched a team charged with improving operating efficiency. The environment was stable. A recent substantial investment in processing facilities assured that the operating environment would remain stable. Customers were nearby manufacturers, and it was unlikely that competitors would be able to lower shipping costs to compete more aggressively. There were no substitute materials on the horizon that might reduce the volume being processed. The team recommended, and management accepted, an incremental-improvement strategy based on the visible opportunities available in each of the departments involved. The team then added 15 percent to each target to ensure that the goal represented a challenge to the operating groups.

Consider what might have happened if this group's environment had been in flux. Had the technology of heat treating been changing rapidly, there might have been no assurance of a stable operating structure on which to base incremental improvements. Had customers been in flux, the volumes on which the expected improvements were founded could not have been trusted. If substitute mate-

---

RULES OF THUMB:
GOAL-SETTING

- The more challenging the goal, the more likely the group will fully engage all of the human resources available.

- The more volatile the environment, the greater the need to favor broad and general goals.

- The more stable the environment, the greater should be the accent on narrow, tight goals and objectives.

---

rial had been on the "radar screen," an investment in refining "old" technology might have been ill advised. Under volatile circumstances, management would probably have accepted more nebulous commitments and commissioned an investigation of a broader range of options.

Group Understanding of Goals and Objectives

Adopting an appropriate mix of broad and narrow objectives framed within a challenging goal is sometimes insufficient. The interpretation of the goals and objectives is information input. That means it is subject to the same potential biases as any other information input. It is important that all team members have the *same understanding* of the goals and objectives as well as the methods by which the goals will be addressed. If they do not, there is a good chance that differing approaches within the team will conflict. If this occurs, unnecessary friction will be generated and its accompanying heat may drain the team's emotional energy.

One method of aligning team members is to have each member paraphrase each group objective in terms of his or her own situation. The team might require that the issue be kept open until all members agree that they can "live" with a particular definition. At the end of this exercise, the team can feel reasonably assured that all members are "pulling the wagon" in roughly the same direction and that group synergy has been roughly maximized.

Ranking Multiple Goals

If a group has multiple goals, the same basic method explained above can be used to rank-order those goals. It is probable that the goals will conflict with one another at specific times and in particular situations. The exercise should help identify those situations.

Also, some members may be able to pursue a particular goal aggressively, while others may be able to address the goal only intermittently. If every member takes a turn rank-ordering the goals in terms of his or her expected contribution, and explains why certain goals were given more weight than others, then the entire group will be advised of one another's circumstances in the context of group objectives. The group will get a "fix" on the expected contribution of each member and possibly figure out how to resolve goal conflicts in a way that benefits everyone.

The purpose of this exercise is not to agree on a single ordering; rather, it is to lay out specific targets and expected contributions. Once those are defined, the group can assess whether achieving the goal is likely considering the rank orderings provided. From a group perspective, it is not necessary that everyone contribute to every goal to the same degree. It is only necessary that the group as a whole realize the objective.

ALLOCATION STRATEGIES

Goals and objectives of a significant nature, whether broad or narrow, are seldom addressed in a single, "all or nothing" stroke. More commonly, they are approached by taking multiple actions over time. Some of these are self-initiated and others are responses to the initiatives of outside agencies.

One major controllable determinant of team success is the ability to allocate the right strategic style to the issue at hand. The initiatives a group generates or receives do not come with a label on them. In any case, group response will be influenced by the strategic postures of group members, and thus information-processing biases will come into play.

Experience has indicated that in this area, two conditions in particular expose group vulnerabilities:

- The more varied the strategic postures in the group, the more likely it is that the initiatives will take divergent trajectories as debates are "won" by one or another faction.

- The more similar the strategic postures in the group, the more likely it is that the preferences of that posture (style or pattern) will be automatically applied to the issue at hand.

Compensating for information-processing biases in allocating strategic styles to initiatives is really just a special case of the process strategy that was addressed earlier. What is needed is a method of systematically compensating for the vulnerability known to be inherent in the group configuration. A structured question strategy of the type outlined in the process section has proven effective in helping groups compensate for these systematic vulnerabilities.

SUBTEAMS

Allocating activities to sub-units of a larger group is another strategy that has proven generally useful in field settings. This mechanism combines the process strategy for identifying the most appropriate approach to a particular issue with the task-structure strategy of constructing the workflow to compensate for a known vulnerability.

Field experience indicates that many groups believe a group must approach all issues as a single entity to qualify as a team. This belief often leads to inefficiency and ineffectiveness—and personally frustrating experiences for everyone involved. It is based on a totally false assumption.

A moment's reflection on the character of most team sports immediately reveals the erroneous nature of this assumption. In most team sports, individuals or groups are assigned specific roles (e.g., defense and offense in football; center and goalie in hockey) and are expected to excel within that capacity. These roles are then combined to form a coordinated whole, which the public then recognizes as a "team." It is common purpose and common destiny that creates a team, and it is unnecessary for every player to be actively involved in every play.

Guidance in this area consists of combining two process strategies:

- The strategy for identifying the most appropriate approach to a particular issue

- A group-composition strategy whereby members whose "natural inclinations" suit the identified approach are selected

In essence, a mini-team is created, one equipped with the strategic styles necessary to address the issue most effectively.

The following case exemplifies the use of the subteam strategy. A large, 16-member team at a telecommunications company had been charged with designing a program for moving the company toward a team-based structure. After six months of meetings focused on this assignment, the team was going nowhere: a condition of near-paralysis had developed.

One of the team's senior members ordered a remote OE analysis of the team. The completed report was distributed to members prior to their next meeting. At the meeting, the person who had ordered the analysis asked if anyone thought that any of the recommendations might have value for the team. Everyone instantly centered on the subteam option. Members had recognized the difficulty the team was having, but needed a systematic method of addressing it. The subteam option provided that method.

The report's outline of this option included a series of questions that the group could use to identify an optimal subteam for a particular issue. The report also suggested that the team use a consensus decision strategy for subteam recommendations. This would be highly feasible because subteams with sufficient overlap in their members' styles could be constructed to accommodate the strategy. The larger team could then review and ratify the subteams' suggestions without having to tangle themselves up in the minutiae that the subteams had already addressed and resolved on a consensus basis.

Members unanimously agreed to adopt this strategy. As a result, the team completed its assignment in six weeks—after six months of paralysis. Such a result, in perhaps less dramatic form, has been repeated many times across many industries, geographic locations, and functions, and at all organizational levels.

Even though the subteam strategy is a combination of other techniques already identified, its wide applicability and material effect warrants its inclusion as a unique guidance mechanism.

OTHER GUIDANCE MECHANISMS

The guidance mechanisms outlined thus far are the ones most generally applicable in field situations; however, many more can be designed to meet special situations. The number and design are limited only by the imaginations of the manager and organizational engineer. Cases in which such guidance mechanisms were used are provided below.

Team Name

Sometimes the simple strategy of assigning a name to a team can prove surprisingly effective. This was the case at a manufacturing plant, with a group assigned to improve the plant's administrative efficiency. The plant manager was involved with the effort, and periodically sent memos to the group. Each member was addressed by name on those memos.

The plant's internal consultant pointed out to the manager that his practice of addressing the memos in this way encouraged the group to look upon the mission as an individual exercise. This kind of approach would inherently limit group gains, since full realization required coordination. The manager agreed, named the team the "Administration Improvement Team," and began addressing his communications accordingly.

As reported by the consultant, there was a perceptible change in attitude among the team members, one that improved subsequent team interactions.

Facilities

An external consultant was charged with installing teams at the maintenance facility of a small power company. The consultant was having difficulty getting one particular group to take the effort seriously. The team members were "old-timers" who had seen past efforts come to naught.

The consultant arranged to have a group meeting in the corporate boardroom. The room was well appointed and conveyed that it was a place where important things happened. The change was instant. Matters that had been frivolously dismissed suddenly became issues of concern. Serious discussion replaced indifference. A temporary change in meeting location thus resulted in a group that was willing and able to make a contribution to the firm.

Sponsorship

A team at a Southwestern chemical company was encountering difficulty moving its agenda forward. The team's charter required the cooperation of other units, but was not getting it. Progress was stalled.

The vice president of the company assigned an internal consultant to help invigorate the effort. The consultant found that the team, which was composed of relatively low-ranking people, was not receiving the cooperation it required from higher-ranking people in other departments. This had repeatedly stalled one or another of the initiatives that the team needed to complete its mission.

The consultant met with the vice president and outlined the difficulty. He had prepared an internal memo from the VP to the team that spoke of the importance of their work and of his personal interest in it. The VP signed the memo on the spot.

The consultant then had the memo sent to the team and advised members that it might be useful to attach a copy of the memo to appropriate internal communications that they issued. They saw merit in the approach and adopted the suggestion.

Momentum picked up immediately. Unreachable executives now found the time to accommodate the team's requests. The VP did nothing beyond signing the memo. It was sufficient that he was known as the sponsor of the effort.

Team Size and Leadership Rotation

Another mechanism that has been used successfully involves operationally reducing the size of large teams by cyclically rotating members; everyone continues to participate, but not all at the same time.

Leadership rotation is yet another possible initiative. In one case, team leadership was rotated to ensure equality of status between team members. Initially, this did not produce desirable results: rotation was done on a weekly basis, and because members had widely varying strategic profiles, each week's work tended to cancel that of prior weeks. However, the solution was simple: to extend the term of leadership to six weeks.

A CLOSING WORD ON FLEXIBLE INITIATIVES

The list of specialized interventions could go on and on. The common thread running through all of these initiatives is that, when properly applied, they produce reasonably predictable patterns of human behavior. They help guide relationships in a way that improves the group's ability to achieve its objectives. None require anyone to "change" or to adopt new beliefs or values. And when they are targeted at the specific conditions of the group, their results are rapid and durable.

A general approach to the selection of guidance interventions is provided in Figure 42, which follows.

Figure 42. Selecting Guidance Interventions

1. Identify the specific information-processing biases of the group. Every group will have them.

2. Identify and/or solidify the group's goals and objectives. Without these, there will be nothing toward which to guide the group.

3. Determine whether the identified goals are shared among group members. If they are not, then there is no common framework in which cooperation can occur.

4. Ensure that all members believe they share a common destiny. If there is no consequence for failure or no benefit to be gained from success, there is no dependable motive for cooperation.

5. Examine the environment fully. High volatility argues for more generalized interventions (e.g., structured questions and roles).

6. Propose more interventions that can be reasonably accepted. Commitment is furthered by the positive involvement of group members in the selection of interventions.

7. Revisit the group over time to monitor for any new conditions. Like any other complex entity, a group requires periodic maintenance to retain full efficiency and effectiveness.

Chapter 7

MATERIALITY
RESULTS THAT MAKE A DIFFERENCE

THE PURPOSE OF UNDERSTANDING, measuring, predicting, and guiding group behavior is to produce results of material significance. When we effectively understand information processing, define a method of accurate measurement, identify a reliable way to predict group behavior, and

DEFINITION REVIEW

➡ **MATERIALITY**
Show that the results of this effort will have a material impact on the issue being addressed

select appropriate guidance mechanisms, we can and should expect tangible, visible improvement in the operation of groups to which it is applied.

The youth of the discipline of organizational engineering precludes wide-scale demonstration of the universal value of the applied paradigm using traditional venues. There simply has not yet been enough time to accumulate rigorous data on wide-scale application or a sufficient number of academically accomplished people to independently assess its effects using commonly acceptable methods.

This is not an unusual condition for seminal theory. For example, Einstein was awarded the Nobel Prize well before the full implications of his theory of relativity were tested in the "real world." The award was based on the compelling logic of his position — it simply had to be true. Similarly, if you found the logic used to develop and define the theory of organizational engineering compelling, you have a legitimate basis on which to draw your own judgement regarding the materiality of the contribution of the new discipline to the field.

A sense of the materiality of organizational engineering can also be gained from the examples included in this book. All were drawn from real life and testify to the applicability of the discipline in "real world" contexts. Stories of the positive consequences of using organizational engineering methodology to groups could easily fill a book of this size. For example, a subsidiary of a large oil firm in upper Michigan was on the verge of selling its assets and going out of business. In the course of two days an internal consultant identified their organizational issues, suggested potential remedies, and went home to Houston. The group of about 60 people took the advice to heart, internally negotiated and reorganized. Within nine months they were on top of the parent company's list of performing subsidiaries and were in the process of acquiring the very firms that, one year before, they had been considering as possible buyers of their firm.

Our Testing Protocols

The protocol used in the development and specification of the theory provides further evidence of the materiality of the approach. The development work was done using a "blind" protocol. Except for the completed organizational engineering survey instrument, no information on the group being analyzed was gathered. Participation was secured by "cold calling" firms and organizations and identifying the person or agency with an interest in organizational effectiveness. That person was then approached and asked to participate using a group with which they had a current interest and activity. The investigator did not know the people sponsoring the analysis or the group to which it was being applied. This protocol left no opportunity for unconscious manipulation or self-deception. The hard copy report provided was either right or wrong, effective or ineffective, accurate or fuzzy.

For the first 500 analyses conducted, every sponsor was recalled and asked for his or her assessment as well as the results realized by the group to which it was applied. The overwhelming majority of the sponsors reported immediately positive results from the application. There was not a single instance of a negative result from the application of the methodology. This initial base provided high confidence that the methodology being applied was effective and that it systematically produced tangible results of observable magnitude.

Since the first 500 evaluations were completed in 1998, recalls were made on about 50 percent of the analyses issued. This practice is ongoing and continues to confirm the value and applicability of organizational engineering theory and methodology. The technology has been applied to well over 1,000 teams and over 10,000 recorded individual results have been captured in the database. Operationally, there is no doubt but that the methods, practices, and processes outlined in this book actually work in real field situations with real people doing real work in real organizations operating in the real economy.

Initial tests of the durability of the interventions have also begun to yield positive results. As reported earlier in this book, an industrial firm in the Midwest conducted a follow-up study and found that 18 months after an intervention, the people involved were still using the insights and the nomenclature of HA, RI, LP, and RS in their daily activity — including at the lunch table. This durability testifies to the value of the theory and processes that underlie the intervention.

The results described above can be described as anecdotal in nature. But then again, scientific proof is merely the organized presentation and evaluation of results that, when considered independently, can be described as anecdotal in nature. The sheer volume of anecdotal results accumulated in the process of developing the discipline of organizational engineering provides a strong degree of evidence of the universal applicability of the theory and practices as outlined in this book.

The reuse of the tools described in the book by teams in field settings further testifies to the materiality of the technology. Some individual teams have returned up to six times to evaluate the addition of new team members or the exit of existing participants. Many more teams have returned two and three times for updates and reassessments. This repeated usage by teams that have already had an initial valuation testifies to the operational value they find in the resultant analysis.

Overall, evidence of a substantial nature has accumulated that testifies to the operational value of organizational engineering. The volume of the evidence is overwhelming. However, the real test of this knowledge is whether it applies to you, in your firm, confronting your issues, and in the context that you deem to be applicable. You are only minutes away from such a practical demonstration of validity and materiality.

Sites on the World Wide Web, including one maintained by the publisher of this volume, are available to provide you with a definitive assessment using the technology described in this book. Test it on yourself and see if the resultant report does not accurately describe your own predispositions and preferences. Try a "One on One" analysis with another person and see if the report does not accurately explain how you interact with that person and identify opportunities and vulnerabilities that you can attest exist in that relationship. Apply it to a group of 10 or 20 people and witness for yourself the accuracy and power of the analysis and recommendations.

In the final analysis, the opinion of an obscure Ph.D. who you do not know is not what counts. What counts is that the knowledge you have acquired really works in your situation, with people whom you know and in a way that meets your criteria of significance. The discipline of organizational engineering has been designed to allow you to conduct your own test, using your own standards. If you have got this far in the book, you have all of the knowledge you need to convince yourself of the value of what you have learned.

SUMMARY

This brief book began with a single, almost self-evident information-processing model. You have been shown how that simple model can be used to predict and guide the behavior of groups toward positive, observable results.

The tool you now have is a new addition to your tool kit of solutions. The book has shown that the primary nature of the mechanisms organizational engineering has identified will "fit" with anything of a higher order level such as the various psychological instruments. It represents a new level of analysis that has always been there but up to now has been invisible without the new lens provided by the theory of organizational engineering.

It replaces nothing and nothing need be discarded to adopt the methodology.

The immediate value of the methodology lies in the fact that it directly addresses the essence of any organizational entity: relationships. Using it you will be able to realize rapid, consistently positive results of a material nature. You now "own" the knowledge. Use it wisely.

Index

Action mode, 10–11, 13, 124
  behavioral range, 21
  measuring, 24
  strategic styles and, 32
  structured method and, 12
  unpatterned method and, 12, 14
Allocation strategies, 128–129
Anecdotal evidence, 140–141
Assessor, 111

Balanced strategic style, 52–53
Behavior. *See also* Group behavior;
  Strategic profiles
  individual, 37–38, 44–46
  markers, 34–35
  method and mode and, 12–14
  prediction. *See* Prediction
  preferences, 69
  range, 26–27
Bidding activity, 116
Brainstorming, 12
Braking role, 112
Bureaucracy, 89

Centroid, 82–84, 85
Changer, 29, 44, 45, 77
Coalitions, 81–84, 98
Commitment, 99
  value of, 94
Common areas, 67–68, 85
  divergent-behavior, 77
  fractal nature, 76–77
  large, 69–71
  no common area, 78–79
  small, 71–73
  why people seek, 68–69
Common axis, 78–79
Consensual agreement, 67–68, 79–81, 99
Consensus area, 92, 94
Consensus rule, 93–95
Consequence, switch mechanism, 49
Conservator, 45, 77
Cost, decision-making, 93–94
Criticizer, 108–109
Cross-functional groups, 89, 98

DecideX, 35
Decision-making, 79–81, 99
  group, 91–95

large common area and, 70
Deliberate behavior, 13
Detailed behavior, 13
Discussion director, 112
Divergent-behavior common area, 77
Dominant strategic style, 84–85
Dutiful behavior, 13

Effectiveness, 90–91
  small common area and, 72
Efficiency, 90
  large common area and, 70
Engineering philosophy, organizational
  engineering, vi
Environment, 98
  goals and, 124–126
  roles and, 110
  rules and, 106–107
  team form and, 89–91
Environmental conditioning, strategic
  style changes and, 55–57
Environmental volatility areas, 91

Facilities, 133
Family, strategic style stability and, 54
Flexible interventions, 88, 101–102,
  135–136
  allocation strategies, 128–129
  facilities, 133
  goals and objectives, 123–128
  knowledge, 116–121
  process, 113–116
  roles, 107–112
  rules, 102–107, 109–110
  sponsorship, 133–134
  subteams, 129–132
  task structure, 121–123
  team name, 132–133
  team size and leadership rotation, 135
Fractals, common areas and, 76–77
Friends, strategic style stability and, 54

Goals, 123–128, 136
  challenging, 123
  environment and, 124–126
  group understanding of, 126–127
  ranking, 127–128
  scope, 123–126
Goal-setting, rules of thumb, 126

Group behavior. *See also* Common areas
  common axis, 78–79
  large groups, 79–81
  mutual agreement, 67–68
  natural coalitions, 81–84
  predicting, 63–64
  rules of thumb, 84–86
  strategic profile identification, 64–65
  trial-and-error initiating, 65–66
  understanding, vi, 1
Group norms, 101, 116
Group performance
  information processing and, 15–16
  organizational engineering and, 16–18
Group vulnerabilities
  process intervention and, 113–116
  task structure and, 121
Group-composition strategy, 130
Groups
  composition, 97–98, 99
  decision methods, 91–95
  size, 96–97, 99
  strategic profile, 92–93
  understanding of goals, 126–127
Guidance, 87–88, 101. *See also* Flexible
    interventions; Semi-fixed interventions
    defined, 87
    organizational engineering and, vii
    selecting interventions, 136

HA. *See* Hypothetical analyzer
Hierarchical method, 92–93, 98–99
Honest broker strategy, 73–76
Hypothetical analyzer (HA), 32, 42–43, 45,
  50–51, 58, 69, 103–104, 106, 108–109,
  122, 124

Ideation, rules to encourage, 104
Individual
  organizational engineering and, 17
  predicting behavior, 37–38, 44–46. *See
  also* Strategic profiles
  roles and, 108–109
  strategic style assessment, 117–120
Inflexibility, rules and, 102–104
Information overload, 6–8
Information processing, 4–5
  biases, 128–129, 136
  filtering input, 6–10
  group performance and, 15–16
  method and mode link, 11–14
  output mode, 10–11

Informational chain, 15–16
Information-processing model, 1
  validity, 2–3
Information-processing theory,
  organizational engineering and, vi–vii
Initialization, 33
Input method, link with mode, 11–14
Inputs, 2–3
  filtering, 4–10
Interests, strategic style stability and, 55
Introductions, 65–66

Keirsey Temperament Sorter, 18
Knowledge, of strategic styles, 116–121

Labeling, strategic styles and, 59–62
Large common areas, 69–71, 85
Large groups, 79–81
Leader, strategic profile, 92–93
Leader–group effects, 93
Leadership rotation, 135
Location, 133
  switch mechanism, 49
Logical behavior, 13
Logical processor (LP), 32, 42, 45, 55–56, 58,
  69, 75, 94, 103–104, 106, 124
LP. *See* Logical processor

Majority area, 92
Majority rule, 93–95, 99
Majority-rule decision-making, 79–81
Materiality
  defined, 137
  organizational engineering and, vii,
  137–143
Matrix, 98
Measurement, 19–22
  behavioral markers, 34–35
  creating operational measure, 22–31
  defined, 19
  organizational engineering and, vii, viii
  steps, 24–31
  tool, 28–31, 60
Method. *See also* Structured method;
Unpatterned method
  continuum, 9
  choosing, 19–22
  filtering input, 8–10
  link with mode, 11–14, 24–26
  organizational, 89
Method-mode options, 21
Mode. *See also* Action mode; Thought

mode
  continuum, 10
  choosing, 19–22
  link with method, 11–14, 24–26
Mutual agreement, 67–68
Myers-Briggs diagnostic, 30–31

Naming
  strategic styles, 31–33, 59–62
  teams, 132–133
Natural coalitions, 81–84
Needle split style, 47–48
Norms, 101, 116

Objectives, 123–128
Occam's Razor, 16–17
OE. See Organizational engineering
Operational scope, small common area
  and, 72
Organizational engineering (OE)
  defined, v
  design parameters, vi–x
  group performance and, 16–18
  instrumentation, 34–35
  psychology and, 16–18
Organizational engineering analysis,
  49–51
Organizational Engineering Institute, Inc.,
  34
Organizational success, strategic profile
  and, 57–59
Organizations, methods and, 89–91
Outcomes, predicting, viii–ix
Output mode, 5, 10–11, 14
  link with method, 11–14

Perfecter, 45, 75
Perfection behavior, 13
Performer, 45, 75, 77, 94
Peripheral styles, 85
Physical, switch mechanism, 49
Potential resolutions, 66
Precise behavior, 13
Prediction, 14, 22–24
  defined, 37
  group behavior, 63–64
  individual behavior, 37–38, 44–46
  organizational engineering and, vii,
    viii–ix
Principle of structural interventions, 88
Process interventions, 113–116
Process strategies, subteams and, 130

Production-oriented behavior, 13
Psychology, organizational engineering
  and, 16–18

Questions, process intervention, 113–116

Ranking, goals, 127–128
Reaction time, 90
Reactive stimulator (RS), 32, 42, 45, 50–51,
  58, 69, 94, 106, 109, 117, 121, 124
Relational innovator (RI), 32, 43, 45, 58, 69,
  75, 103, 106, 108, 109, 112, 117, 124
Relationships
  organizational engineering and, 63
  roles and, 107–112
  seating arrangements and, 88
Response mode, 14
Review process, 116
RI. See Relational innovator
Risk taking, rules to encourage, 105
Risk-averse behavior, 13
Roles, 107–109
  characteristics, 107
  constructing, 110–112
  rules and, 109–110
RS. See Reactive stimulator
Rules, 102–107
  characteristics, 103
  roles and, 109–110

Seating arrangements, 88
Self-directed teams, 89
Semi-fixed interventions, 88
  decision methods, 91–95
  group composition, 97–98
  group form, 89–91
  group size, 96–97
  rules of thumb, 98–99
Signaling mechanism, 50–51
Size
  group, 96–97, 99
  team, 135
Skeptical behavior, 13
Small common areas, 71–73, 85
Social, switch mechanism, 49
Social constraint
  choice and, 21–22
  exercise, 23
Specialization, 54
  choice and, 20–21
Specifier, 111
Split patterns, 85

Split strategic style, 46–52
Split styles, 85
  group profile, 94–95
Split-style signals, 50–51
Split-style switches, 48–49
Sponsorship, 133–134
Stability, strategic style, 54–55
Standard Graphic, 28–31, 60
Strategic patterns, 43–46
  rules of thumb, 85–86
Strategic profiles, 38–40. *See also* Common
    areas
  centroid, 82–84
  determining probable response, 40–46
  identification, 64–65
  organizational success, 57–59
  problematic profiles, 46–53
  sample, 39
  similarity in, 81–82
Strategic style changes, 53–55
  environmental conditioning and, 55–57
Strategic styles, 15–16, 25–28
  balanced, 52–53
  contingency table, 68
  knowledge of, 116–121
  labeling issues, 59–62
  naming, 31–33
  rules of thumb, 84–86
  value attribution and, 30–31, 33
  split, 46–52
  strength of, 40–43
Strength of style, 40–43
Structural adjustments, vii
Structural interventions, 87–88
Structured action, 25–28
Structured group forms, 90–91
Structured method, 9, 11–12, 13
  behavioral range, 21
  measuring, 24
  organization and, 89–91
  strategic styles and, 32
Structured thought, 25–28
Style preferences, 40–43
Subgroups, 97
Subordinate, signaling strategy, 51
Subteams, 129–132
Superior, signaling strategy, 51
Super-majority methods, 79
Switch mechanisms, 48–49
Synergy, 71, 73, 75–76

Task structure, 121–123
Tasks, group size and, 97, 99
Teams, 89–91, 98
  name, 132–133
  size, 135
Tenacious behavior, 13
Testing protocols, organizational
    engineering, 139–142
Thought mode, 10–11, 13, 124
  behavioral range, 21
  measuring, 24
  strategic styles and, 32
  structured method and, 12
  unpatterned method, 12–14
Trial-and-error initiating, 65–66

Understanding, vi
  defined, 1
Unhurried behavior, 13
Unpatterned action, 25–28
Unpatterned group forms, 90, 98
Unpatterned method, 9, 12–14
  behavioral range, 21
  measuring, 24
  organization and, 89–91
  strategic styles and, 32
Unpatterned strategies
  roles and, 109
  rules and, 106
Unpatterned thought, 25–28

Value attribution, 30–31, 33, 59–62
Venturer, 112

Work, strategic style stability and, 54
Work groups, 89, 98
World Wide Web, organizational
    engineering and, 141

Zone of agreement, 67